First published in Great Britain
in 2016 by Hodder & Stoughton
An Hachette UK company

1

A CIP catalogue record for this title is available
from the British Library

Hardback ISBN 978 1 473 65143 2
Ebook ISBN 978 1 473 65142 5

Editorial Director: Nicky Ross
Project Editor: Sarah Hammond
Copy Editor: Anne Sheasby
Editor: Helena Caldon
Designer & Art Director: Nathan Burton
Photographer: Jamie Orlando Smith
Food Stylist: Phil Mundy
Props Stylist: Olivia Wardle

Typeset in Avenir and Archer

Printed and bound in Germany
by Mohn Media GmbH

Hodder & Stoughton policy is to use papers that
are natural, renewable and recyclable products and
made from wood grown in sustainable forests. The
logging and manufacturing processes are expected
to conform to the environmental regulations of the
country of origin.

Hodder & Stoughton Ltd
Carmelite House
50 Victoria Embankment
London EC4Y 0DZ

www.hodder.co.uk

# BREAD STREET

## KITCHEN

# GORDON RAMSAY

### and the
### Bread Street Kitchen Team

HODDER &
STOUGHTON

# CONTENTS

Bread Street Kitchen is open all day, every day, for breakfast, lunch and dinner, and I really enjoy seeing the atmosphere change through the different mealtimes. With the restaurant being in the City, the early morning vibe during the working week is quite serious and high-powered, whereas weekend brunches tend to be lazy, relaxed affairs that go on all morning. I love the buzz of the weekday lunch service as the noise levels pick up and the pressure on the kitchen intensifies for a couple of hours, but I also like the less-frenzied pace of Sunday lunches when families and local residents replace the City workers and people stay for longer. Evenings are different again – the bar comes alive, the lights go down, corks are popped and the focus is on having a really good time. I don't think I've ever seen the restaurant empty – there's always someone drinking coffee or sipping a glass of something at the bar. Whatever the time of day, Bread Street Kitchen is open for business.

When it came to planning the BSK menu, we wanted the focus to be on top-quality seasonal produce cooked with passion. Given our location, next to St Paul's Cathedral in the oldest part of London, there had to be some British classics, but they sit alongside international dishes from Europe, Asia and beyond. We had to include some sharing platters, too, not to mention a

wood-fired oven, a killer cocktail list and great bar snacks… but ultimately, we just wanted the restaurant to be somewhere that people could come along to at any time of the day and always find something that they really wanted to eat.

This ethos of good food whenever you want it is what we wanted to capture in this book. These days, we seem to be busier than ever, but we each make time to cook for different reasons. You might want to start making more nourishing breakfasts for yourself or perhaps invite a big group of friends over for a weekend feast. You might need inspiration for everyday suppers or new ideas for entertaining. Or you might, like many of us, simply cook for pleasure and want to discover new ways to indulge your passion.

So here we have put together a collection of recipes that are perfect for morning, noon and night and the bits in-between; there is something for everyone whatever the time of day. Because cooking is something we often do for friends and family, there are lots of ideas for social gatherings, like brunch, weekend lunches and special dinners. But there is plenty of inspiration for breakfasts and simple midweek suppers too. This food reflects the way we live our lives right now and I hope these recipes make you want to get stuck in.

Gordon Ramsay

# Cooking the Bread Street Kitchen way

We know that cooking in a restaurant is very different from cooking at home, but there are a few tricks and tips that you can pick up from professional chefs that will improve your own cooking. Our Bread Street recipes have been tweaked for this book so that you can make them in a home kitchen, but we haven't changed the methods much so you will be preparing these dishes almost exactly as we do, with delicious tried-and-tested results.

For all the differences between professional and domestic cooking, there are some things that should always be the same, of course. For example, always try to source the best ingredients you can – your cooking will only ever be as good as the ingredients you use, so make sure they are of good quality. Also, food will always taste better when it is in season – there is nothing much you can do to make a woolly February tomato taste like a sweet, ripe August one. We also think that respect for animal welfare and sustainable fishing methods should go without saying – but we're going to say it anyway!

# Cook's Notes

### Animal welfare
Please choose free-range eggs and chickens and ensure that all meat comes from animals that have led happy lives.

### Fish
Always buy fish and shellfish that have been caught, harvested or farmed in a sustainable way.

### Eggs
All eggs are medium in these recipes unless otherwise specified.

### Butter
We use unsalted butter for cooking in the restaurant kitchen so that we can control the overall seasoning of the dish. Use whatever you have, but if you cook with salted butter, the dish might need less seasoning later. So always taste it before adding more salt.

### Cooking oil
We use flavourless vegetable oil for high-temperature cooking, but you could use rapeseed or groundnut oil instead. We also cook with olive oil, but more often save the really good-quality extra virgin olive oil for drizzling over finished dishes and in salad dressings.

### Oven temperatures
Our ovens are electric fan ovens, but we have also given the equivalent temperatures for conventional and gas ovens. All ovens are different, though, so get to know yours for the best results.

# GET GOING

Bread Street Kitchen is in the heart of the City, where the day starts early for the many workers in Britain's financial sector. We open our doors at 7am, an hour before the London Stock Exchange starts trading, and our breakfast menu is full of tempting (and mostly healthy) ways to start the working day. Alongside the essential full English and cooked breakfast options are lots of delicious dishes that are designed to fill you up and keep you going until lunch.

We all know that breakfast is the most important meal of the day and that skipping it is a really bad idea. In fact, they say that those who skip breakfast go on to snack more during the day, find it less easy to concentrate and, more worryingly, increase their risk of developing various long-term health problems such as diabetes and heart disease. And yet many of us rush off to work, go to the gym or do the school run without consuming anything more than a cup of tea or coffee. We make it easy for workers to get to the office ready to start the day, but we appreciate that mornings at home are just as busy and rushed and that convenience often wins out when time is short. However, we also know that with a bit of forethought and organisation quick breakfasts can be nutritious ones – and vice versa. For example, soaking Bircher muesli in almond milk the night before means that it is ready to go as soon as you get out of bed. Similarly, making a large batch of our nutty granola means having your own healthy cereal on hand whenever you need it – just add milk or yoghurt and some fresh berries.

Some of our breakfast recipes are a little more involved, but taking a bit of time a couple of days a week, or even on a lazy weekend morning, in order to feed yourself and your family properly will be very satisfying and nourishing. You can make our buttermilk pancakes for the kids and send them off to school happy in the knowledge that they are full of energy for the day ahead. Or you can fuel up with a protein-packed cheese and mushroom omelette, or smash yourself an avocado to serve with warm toast and a couple of poached eggs to linger over with the newspaper. But even if you only have time to whip up a fresh fruit and vegetable juice to drink along with your usual Marmite on toast before you rush out of the door, you can feel satisfied that it will contribute to your five-a-day and give you a great vitamin boost, too.

So start the day as you mean to go on and get into the habit of treating yourself to a proper brekkie before you leave the house.

# GET GOING

# Bircher muesli

There is something so satisfying about going to bed knowing that you have already made your breakfast for the following morning, especially when it is good for you, too. The combination of oats, nuts and seeds in this muesli provides slow-releasing energy that will keep you feeling full all morning. If there are any ingredients you don't like, swap them for ones that you prefer – such as hazelnuts, walnuts, pumpkin seeds, linseeds or dried apricots. You can soak the muesli in different milks, too – try soya, rice or oat milk instead of almond or cow's milk.

1. Tip the oats, raisins, sunflower seeds, almonds, goji berries, chia seeds and cinnamon into a bowl and mix everything together. If you wish, the mix can be transferred to an airtight container at this stage (see Tip) for later.

2. When you are ready to serve, divide the muesli among two bowls (remember it will swell when the liquid is added). Mix together the milk and vanilla extract in a jug, then pour half of it over each portion of muesli. Cover the bowls with cling film and leave to soak in the fridge overnight.

3. The next day, stir the Bircher muesli, then drizzle each portion with a little honey (if using) to sweeten and scatter the mixed berries on top to serve.

SERVES 2

100g porridge oats

25g raisins

25g sunflower seeds

15g flaked almonds

10g goji berries

1 tsp chia seeds

Pinch of ground cinnamon

400ml unsweetened almond milk, or whole or semi-skimmed milk

Few drops of vanilla extract

*To serve*

Runny honey, for drizzling (optional)

Blueberries and raspberries

TIP
This recipe can easily be multiplied, as it keeps well in an airtight container or sealed jar. If you do store it, one dry portion weighs about 60g.

# Porridge

*with apple and cinnamon compote*

Waking up to a bowl of warming porridge really sets you up for the day ahead. To be healthier, you can make the porridge with skimmed milk or even water, but in the restaurant we use whole milk and double cream, which makes it a wonderfully indulgent treat. If you don't have time to make the apple compote, stir through a dollop of raspberry jam or a spoonful of honey for sweetness.

1. First make the compote. Place all the ingredients in a pan with 2 tablespoons of water, cover and cook gently for about 20 minutes, until the apples have cooked down and softened. Stir the mixture halfway through to make sure it's cooking evenly.

2. Meanwhile, make the porridge. Pour the milk and cream into a separate pan, and bring to a simmer. Put the oats into a heatproof bowl, then pour over the hot milk and cream, stirring continuously.

3. Return the mixture to the pan and cook gently for 5–10 minutes, stirring constantly, until the porridge is cooked and is a nice thick consistency. Add a splash of water, if you want to loosen it once it's cooked. Season with a pinch of salt.

4. Serve the porridge with the warm compote spooned on top.

SERVES 4

*For the porridge*
600ml whole milk
200ml double cream (see Tip)
200g porridge oats
Pinch of sea salt

*For the apple and cinnamon compote*

3 dessert apples, such as Braeburn, peeled, cored and roughly chopped
30g light muscovado sugar
30g sultanas or raisins
1 tsp ground cinnamon

TIP
Use extra milk in place of the cream, if you prefer.

# Granola

The beauty of making your own granola is that you can add the seeds that you really like, plus you can make it more or less sweet, if you prefer. The BSK granola is ideal to make in a large batch and can be stored in an airtight container for up to two weeks. It is particularly delicious served with natural yoghurt and fresh fruit for breakfast but it can also be eaten as a snack on its own or sprinkled over ice cream to add a delicious crunch.

1. Preheat the oven to 200°C/180°C fan/Gas 6.

2. Mix together the oats, pumpkin seeds, sesame seeds and cinnamon in a bowl. In a separate bowl, mix together the vegetable oil, maple syrup, golden syrup and honey.

3. Combine the dry and wet ingredients, mixing them together using your hands. Transfer the mixture to a large roasting tray, pressing down lightly so it's flat and even.

4. Bake for 30 minutes, until crisp and golden, stirring the mixture at least once during baking.

5. Remove from the oven and sprinkle with the desiccated coconut, then bake for a further 5–10 minutes until lightly toasted.

6. Set aside to cool, then serve or store in an airtight container until needed. Serve with plain yoghurt and some fresh fruit, such as pears, plums, mango or mixed berries.

SERVES 10

320g jumbo oats

50g pumpkin seeds

50g sesame seeds

1 tbsp ground cinnamon

40ml vegetable oil

70g maple syrup

25g golden syrup

25g runny honey

2 tbsp desiccated coconut

Plain yoghurt and chopped pears and plums, to serve

# Buttermilk pancakes

*with blueberries and maple syrup*

These light and fluffy American-style pancakes are a great way to feed hungry children (and adults!) as they are moreish and filling without being too sweet. You can top them with any seasonal fresh fruit (blueberries are especially good), or serve them with crispy smoked bacon and maple syrup for that classic salty/sweet combination.

1. Sift the flour, baking powder and salt into a large bowl, add the sugar and mix together. Make a well in the middle and tip in the egg yolks. Gradually add the buttermilk and whisk slowly, bringing the flour in from the edges until it is all combined. Whisk in the oil and vanilla extract until combined.

2. In a separate grease-free bowl, whisk the egg whites until they form soft peaks, then fold them evenly into the batter.

3. Heat a wide, non-stick frying pan over a medium heat. Add a dash of oil and a knob or two of the butter. Once the butter has melted, cook the pancakes in batches of four at a time, using 1 heaped tablespoon of batter per pancake. Shape each pancake into a round disc in the pan. Cook over a medium heat for 2–3 minutes, turning once, until golden brown on each side. Keep warm in a low oven while you repeat with the remaining batter, adding a little extra oil and a knob or two of butter for each batch.

4. To serve, divide the pancakes among serving plates, then sprinkle generously with the blueberries and top with a drizzle of maple syrup.

SERVES 4-6 (MAKES 12 SMALL PANCAKES)

160g plain flour

2 tsp baking powder

Pinch of sea salt

1 tbsp caster sugar

2 large eggs, separated

300ml buttermilk

4 tbsp vegetable oil, plus extra for frying

1 tsp vanilla extract

50g butter, for frying

150g blueberries

Maple syrup, to serve

# Avocado and toast
*with poached eggs*

You can't eat out for breakfast these days without seeing avocado and toast on the menu, so here is our zesty version, which has fresh orange pieces and semi-dried cherry tomatoes mixed in. Pepped up with chilli flakes, topped with poached eggs and finished with flaked almonds, this breakfast dish is guaranteed to get your day off to a fantastic start.

1. Peel the orange and break into segments, removing any seeds and as much pith as possible. Chop the segments into small pieces and place in a bowl with any juice.

2. Halve the avocado, then remove the stone and peel off the skin. Roughly chop the flesh, then add it to the orange along with the semi-dried tomatoes, chilli flakes and salt. Stir roughly to combine, then cover and set aside.

3. Poach the eggs. Bring a saucepan of water to a gentle simmer and add the vinegar. Break an egg into a teacup or ramekin, then whisk the water to create a gentle whirlpool and tip the egg into the centre of it. Leave to cook for 3 minutes, or until the egg floats to the top and the white is cooked but the yolk still soft. Lift the egg out with a slotted spoon and drain on kitchen paper. Keep warm while you cook the remaining egg in the same way.

4. Meanwhile, toast the almonds in a small, dry frying pan over a medium heat for a few minutes, until golden brown, shaking the pan regularly to prevent burning. Set aside. In the meantime, toast the bread on both sides then place on a serving plate.

5. Serve the avocado mixture alongside the two slices of toast, topped with the poached eggs and scattered with the toasted almonds and extra chilli flakes.

SERVES 1

1 small orange

1 medium ripe avocado

5 semi-dried cherry tomato
    halves
Pinch of dried chilli flakes, plus
    extra to serve

Pinch of sea salt

Dash of white wine vinegar

2 eggs

2 tsp flaked almonds

2 slices of sourdough bread

# Wild mushroom and Gruyère omelette

For this great breakfast omelette, try to use fresh wild mushrooms that are in season, as they will always give the best flavour. Ceps (or porcini) are in season from August to November and are particularly good, or try a mixture of edible wild varieties. It is also wonderfully decadent to treat yourself to a few shavings of truffle scattered over the omelette just before serving. The cream makes this already indulgent omelette even more so, but you can leave it out if you prefer a leaner start to the day.

1. Preheat the grill to medium.

2. Whisk the eggs and cream (if using) together in a small bowl.

3. Melt the butter in a 20cm grill-proof, non-stick frying pan over a medium–high heat. Add the mushrooms and sauté until nicely coloured, about 4 minutes.

4. Reduce the heat slightly, pour in the beaten egg mixture, then quickly fold in the Gruyère cheese, bringing the raw mixture in from the sides of the pan. Season with salt and pepper, then sprinkle over the parsley.

5. Cook on the hob for a couple of minutes, without stirring, until the omelette is lightly browned underneath. Place the omelette under the hot grill and grill for about 2 minutes, until golden and puffed up.

6. Transfer the omelette to a serving plate and serve immediately with the dressed rocket.

SERVES 1

3 large eggs

50ml double cream (optional)

25g butter

100g mixed wild mushrooms, cleaned and sliced

40g Gruyère cheese, grated

1 tbsp roughly chopped fresh parsley leaves

Sea salt and freshly ground black pepper

Rocket, lightly dressed in extra virgin olive oil, to serve

# Green machine

Making a green juice with fresh fruit and spinach for breakfast is a quick and easy way to give yourself a healthy boost first thing in the morning, plus it adds to your five-a-day. Invest in a good blender and try different combinations of fruits, vegetables, leaves and seeds each time.

1. Peel, core and roughly chop the pear. Peel the kiwi, cut off one slice and set it aside, then quarter the rest of the fruit.

2. Put the prepared fruit into a blender with the mint and spinach leaves. Pour in the apple juice.

3. Blend together until smooth, then pour into a tall glass, slit the kiwi slice, pop it on the side of the glass and serve immediately.

SERVES 1

1 pear

1 kiwi

1 mint sprig, leaves only

Small handful of spinach, rinsed

125ml apple juice

# Berry boost

Summer berries such as strawberries, raspberries and blueberries are full of vitamins and antioxidants, and this colourful combination is bright, zesty and refreshing. You can also use frozen fruit all year round for a much-needed taste of summer on those chilly winter mornings.

1. Put the strawberries, raspberries and blueberries into a blender. Pour in the orange and apple juices, add the picked mint leaves and blitz together. Squeeze in the lemon juice and mix.

2. Pour into a glass and serve immediately with a mint sprig.

SERVES 1

4 strawberries, quartered

10 raspberries

Handful of blueberries

50ml orange juice

50ml apple juice

3 mint sprigs, leaves picked from 2

Juice of ½ lemon

BRUNCH

We are big fans of the late breakfast/early lunch at Bread Street. Our weekend brunches are lazy affairs when the pace in the restaurant (and in the City streets outside) slows right down. People can linger over their eggs Benedict and Sunday papers while treating themselves to a bespoke Bloody Mary or an umpteenth glass of Prosecco from the bar. The morning gently rolls into the afternoon and no one is in a hurry.

But you don't have to go to a restaurant for brunch… you can turn weekend breakfasts at home into special occasions by inviting friends over or cooking together as a family. On the menu should be brunch classics such as French toast with crispy bacon and maple syrup, Spicy scrambled eggs or Sweetcorn fritters. The cooking should be relaxed and the presentation laidback. Portion sizes should be generous and if there

has been some partying the night before, go for bold flavours and nourishing comfort food. We obviously wouldn't want to encourage drinking at home in the morning but we've heard that a big jug of Bloody Mary is just the thing to see off any lingering hangovers…

Brunch can be romantic, too, and you don't even have to get dressed to cook it. Treat the one you love to a special breakfast in bed accompanied by a glass of our signature Buck's Fizz. You will earn enough Brownie points to last a year! Our British lobster roll is particularly indulgent and can even be taken on a mid-morning picnic if you're ever that organised at the weekend to plan one.

Whatever you cook and wherever you serve it, take your time – brunch is a meal that should never be rushed.

# BRUNCH

| | |
|---|---|
| Spicy scrambled eggs | 37 |
| French toast | 38 |
| *with bacon or berries* | |
| Sweetcorn and green chilli fritters | 41 |
| *with red pepper relish and avocado* | |
| British lobster rolls | 42 |
| *with Marie Rose sauce* | |
| Ricotta hotcakes | 45 |
| *with bananas and stem ginger butter* | |
| BSK Bloody Mary | 46 |
| Buck's Fizz Mary | 46 |

# Spicy scrambled eggs

These spicy scrambled eggs are definitely worth getting out of bed for… hot, smoky and creamy all at the same time, they are perfect for seeing you through the morning after the night before. Serve large spoonfuls on toast or with bread to mop up all the tasty juices.

1. Slowly cook the chorizo in a large frying pan for about 5 minutes, until caramelised and the red oil has come out. Remove the chorizo from the pan, but make sure you leave all of the oil in the pan (this will help to flavour the scrambled eggs).

2. Add the onion, chilli and smoked paprika to the pan, and cook over a medium–low heat until the onion is soft, about 5 minutes.

3. Add the butter, eggs and milk, mixing with a plastic spatula, then cook gently, stirring constantly, until the eggs are light, fluffy and cooked to your liking.

4. Stir in the fried chorizo, spring onions, tomato, most of the parsley and Comté cheese to finish, then remove from the heat.

5. Season with salt, sprinkle with the remaining parsley and serve with toasted sourdough bread.

100g spicy cooking chorizo, diced

1 small white onion, sliced

1 red chilli, deseeded and finely chopped

2 tsp smoked paprika

25g butter

12 large eggs

50ml whole milk

8 spring onions, trimmed and finely sliced

1 small ripe tomato, diced

A handful of chopped fresh flat leaf parsley

50g Comté cheese, grated

Sea salt

Toasted sourdough bread, to serve

# French toast

## *with bacon or berries*

French toast (often known as eggy bread), a brunch classic, can either be savoury or sweet, depending on your mood. This clever way of cooking bacon is how we manage to make it so flat and crispy in the restaurant, but it won't work for back bacon; it has to be streaky rashers because they are so finely sliced and have more fat running through them. For the sweet version, use seasonal mixed berries of your choice.

1. For the savoury version, preheat the oven to 190°C/170°C fan/ Gas 5.

2. Lay the bacon rashers on a baking tray, then place a second baking tray on top. Cook in the oven for 15–20 minutes or until the bacon is completely crisp.

3. Meanwhile, for the French toast, lightly whisk the milk and eggs together in a mixing bowl. For the savoury version, season with the salt and pepper.

4. Place the bread slices into the egg mixture and leave them to soak for 30 seconds or so on either side, turning once (the bread slices only need a brief soak, so they don't become too soggy and fall apart).

5. Heat the butter and oil in a large, non-stick frying pan over a medium heat until melted. Add two slices of egg-soaked bread and cook for 1–2 minutes on each side, turning once, until golden brown all over. Remove to serving plates and keep warm. Repeat twice with the remaining egg-soaked bread slices, adding a little extra butter and oil, if needed.

6. Remove the bacon from the oven and drain on kitchen paper. Serve the savoury French toast with the crispy smoked bacon on top and drizzle with maple syrup.

7. For the sweet version, prepare the French toast as above, adding the sugar, honey or maple syrup, vanilla extract and salt to the egg mixture, before soaking the bread slices. Cook as in step 5, then serve with a dollop of ricotta or crème fraîche, some fresh berries and a drizzle of maple syrup or jam.

SERVES 6

*For the French toast*

130ml whole milk

3 eggs

6 thick slices of white bread (or other bread of your choice), crusts removed

½ tsp butter

1 tsp vegetable oil

*For the savoury version*

12 rashers of smoked streaky bacon

Pinch of sea salt

Pinch of freshly ground black pepper

Maple syrup, to serve

*For the sweet version*

2 tbsp caster sugar, runny honey or maple syrup

1 tsp vanilla extract

¼ tsp sea salt

250g ricotta or reduced-fat crème fraîche, to serve

Fresh berries, to serve

Maple syrup or jam, to serve

# Sweetcorn and green chilli fritters
## with red pepper relish and avocado

This is a Bread Street Kitchen brunch favourite. The combination of sweetcorn, hot chilli and cool crème fraîche is unbeatable, especially when served with a dollop of avocado and our very own red pepper relish. Adding lemon juice to the avocado will prevent it going brown while you cook the fritters, and the relish can be made in advance. In fact, why not make a double batch and keep the extra in the fridge to serve with cooked chicken, steak or sausages, or to accompany your favourite cheese and crackers?

1. First make the relish. Preheat the oven to 220°C/200°C fan/Gas 7. Preheat the grill to high. Line a baking tray with baking parchment.

2. Lay the pepper halves, cut side down, on the baking tray. Roast for 15 minutes, then add the tomatoes to the tray and roast together for a further 15 minutes, until the tomatoes have burst and are softened, and the pepper is well charred. Set the tomatoes aside. Place the peppers in a freezer bag, seal and cool for 5–10 minutes, then remove from the bag, peel off the skin and dice the flesh.

3. Meanwhile, heat the oil in a pan, add the onion and sauté over a medium heat until very soft and tinged brown, about 6–8 minutes.

4. Add the roasted pepper and cherry tomatoes, along with any of their juices, to the onion in the pan, then cook over a medium heat for a couple of minutes or so, until the mixture cooks down and thickens to a relish consistency. Leave to cool to room temperature before serving.

5. Next prepare the avocado. Peel and stone the avocados, then roughly chop the flesh and place in a food processor. Add the lemon juice and seasoning, then blend to a rough purée, or whizz until smooth, if you prefer. Cover and chill until ready to serve.

6. For the fritters, mix the flour, baking powder, salt and some pepper in a bowl. Gradually beat in the eggs, then the milk to make a smooth batter. Stir in the sweetcorn, spring onions, chilli and coriander.

7. Fry the fritters in batches in a large, non-stick frying pan. Heat the pan over a medium–high heat with a knob of butter and when it is sizzling, spoon in ½ ladleful of batter per fritter, patting into shape. Fry for 2–3 minutes until golden, then flip over and repeat on the other side. Remove and keep warm while you cook the remaining fritters.

8. To serve, top each hot fritter with a spoonful of the red pepper relish, avocado and crème fraîche.

MAKES ABOUT 8 LARGE (10CM) FRITTERS (*serve 1 fritter plus accompaniments per person*)

*For the red pepper relish*
1 red pepper, halved and deseeded
300g cherry tomatoes
2 tbsp olive oil
1 red onion, finely sliced

*For the avocado*
2 ripe avocados
4 tsp lemon juice
Sea salt and freshly ground black pepper

*For the fritters*
90g plain flour
1½ tsp baking powder
½ tsp sea salt
3 large eggs, beaten
4 tbsp whole milk
400g sweetcorn, tinned or frozen (thawed), drained and patted dry on kitchen paper
6 spring onions, trimmed and finely sliced
1 large green chilli, deseeded and finely diced
2 tbsp chopped fresh coriander, plus extra leaves to serve
About 30g butter, for frying
Crème fraîche, to serve

TIP
The relish can be made several days ahead, cooled, then stored in a covered bowl in the fridge.

# British lobster rolls

*with Marie Rose sauce*

What could be more decadent than lobster for breakfast? Serve this on Valentine's Day, Christmas morning or a special anniversary for a truly impressive romantic brunch. If you are daunted by the thought of cooking a live lobster, you can always buy one pre-cooked and mix it with the classic retro sauce. Not feeling flush? This recipe works very well with cooked prawns, too. Champagne is essential, though.

1. Put the live lobster into the freezer for about 2 hours to put it to sleep.

2. Fill a large saucepan with cold water and add the lemon juice, salt, thyme sprigs and bay leaf, then bring to the boil. Add the lobster to the pan, cover with a lid, then bring to the boil over a medium heat.

3. When the water is just boiling, reduce the heat and simmer for about 10 minutes, until the lobster turns pink. Remove the lobster from the pan and leave it to cool slightly. Discard the water and herbs.

4. Once the lobster is cool enough to handle, pull the head and body apart. Crack the claws using the back of a heavy knife and carefully remove the flesh, keeping it as whole as possible. Set aside. Crack the shell on the tail and pull the flesh out in one piece. Slice the flesh into even-sized chunks, then place in a bowl and set aside.

5. Mix together all of the ingredients for the Marie Rose sauce in a bowl and season with salt and pepper. Add the chopped lobster flesh to the sauce and stir until well coated.

6. Preheat the grill to medium. Warm the bread rolls under the grill, then slice lengthways and load up each one with a couple of slices of tomato, some shredded lettuce and the dressed lobster. Sprinkle with a little paprika. Serve immediately with a glass of Champagne.

SERVES 2

1 live native lobster,
    about 500–600g

Juice of 1 lemon

Large pinch of sea salt

4 thyme sprigs

1 bay leaf

2 soft white bread rolls, halved

1 plum tomato, sliced

½ little gem lettuce, shredded

Smoked paprika, for seasoning

*For the Marie Rose sauce*

3 tbsp mayonnaise

1 tbsp tomato ketchup

Dash of Worcestershire sauce

Squeeze of lemon juice

2 tsp brandy

Dash of Tabasco sauce

Sea salt and freshly ground
    black pepper

# Ricotta hotcakes
*with bananas and stem ginger butter*

Our hotcakes really do sell like their proverbial cousins… Made with ricotta to make them light and tasty, these pancakes are never off the menu. You could just drizzle them with runny honey or maple syrup but making the butter is really easy and the results are spectacular. Stem ginger is widely available in supermarkets and keeps for a long time for use in cakes and other bakes.

1. First make the stem ginger butter. Put the butter, maple syrup and stem ginger into a small bowl and mix together using a spatula until smooth and combined. Cover and set aside while you make the hotcakes.

2. Put the ricotta, milk and egg yolks into a mixing bowl and beat together just until combined using a balloon whisk. Sift the flour, baking powder and salt together, then gradually beat this into the egg yolk mixture until smooth and combined.

3. In a separate large, grease-free bowl, whisk the egg whites until they form stiff peaks. Carefully fold half of the whisked whites into the batter, then fold in the remaining half until evenly combined but the mixture is still light and fluffy.

4. Melt a knob of the butter in a large, non-stick frying pan over a low–medium heat until foaming. Cook the hotcakes in batches over a medium heat (adjusting the heat if necessary so the butter doesn't burn), using 2 tablespoons of batter per hotcake (you can cook two or three at once, but don't overcrowd the pan). After spooning in the batter for each hotcake, gently spread each one with the back of the spoon to make a circle about 8–10cm diameter. Fry for 1–2 minutes until golden brown, then flip the hotcakes and repeat on the other side. Remove to a plate and keep warm while you cook the remaining hotcakes.

5. Serve the warm hotcakes topped with dollops of the stem ginger butter and the banana slices.

SERVES 4–6 (MAKES ABOUT 14 HOTCAKES)

*For the hotcakes*
250g ricotta
150ml whole milk
3 large eggs, separated
75g plain flour
¾ tsp baking powder
Pinch of sea salt
30g butter, for frying

*For the stem ginger butter*
60g butter, at room temperature
2–3 tbsp maple syrup
2 large balls of stem ginger in syrup (about 40g in total, drained weight), drained and finely chopped

2 bananas, sliced on the diagonal, to serve

TIP
Use the batter when freshly made so that it doesn't lose its fluffiness, otherwise it may deflate a bit on standing.

# BSK Bloody Mary

Weekend brunch wouldn't be complete without a Bloody Mary, but when it comes to the perfect combination of ingredients, there is much debate. This is our house spice mix and we think it's hard to beat. Make up a batch and simply mix with vodka and tomato juice for the ultimate mid-morning tipple.

1. Put all the ingredients for the spice mix into a blender and blitz together until smooth. Pour into a sterilised bottle or jar, seal and store in the fridge for up to 5 days.

2. To make each Bloody Mary, add 2–3 teaspoons of the spice mix to the vodka and tomato juice, stirring to combine. Pour into a glass over ice (if using) and serve straightaway.

MAKES ABOUT 310ML (*Serves 20-30, serving 2-3 tsp per drink*)

*For the spice mix*
2 fresh basil leaves
½ rosemary sprig, leaves stripped
½ celery stick, trimmed
2 pitted green olives
1 green chilli, deseeded
½ shallot, roughly chopped
½ tsp paprika
½ tsp cayenne pepper
½ tsp black peppercorns
½ tsp garlic salt
½ tsp Dijon mustard
½ tsp horseradish sauce
250ml Worcestershire sauce

*For each Bloody Mary*
2–3 tsp BSK Bloody Mary Spice Mix
 (*see above*)
1 shot of vodka (25ml) (see Tip)
150ml fresh tomato juice
Ice cubes, to serve (optional)

TIP
For a delicious Virgin Mary, simply omit the vodka.

# Buck's Fizz Mary

This is Buck's Fizz with a Bread Street twist. The fresh ginger and orange vodka added to the classic combination of fresh orange juice and sparkling wine make it spicy and warming – perfect for Christmas morning or Boxing Day brunch. The quantities are easily doubled or tripled if serving to a gathering of friends and family.

1. Mix together the vodka, orange juice and ginger juice in a jug, then pour into the bottom of two Champagne flutes.

2. Fill the glasses with Champagne or Prosecco and give each a quick stir before serving.

SERVES 2

50ml orange or mandarin vodka
40ml orange juice
20ml ginger juice (see Tip)
Champagne or Prosecco, to serve

TIP
For the ginger juice, grate a thumb-sized piece of fresh root ginger, then press it through a small sieve, collecting the juice in a bowl underneath.

# LUNCH

At Bread Street, lunch is a busy, noisy affair as workers, shoppers and tourists flood in to eat. We regularly serve 250 people on a weekday – and all between 12 and 2pm. Though there are always some people who can linger, most diners are rushing back to their desks or want to get on with their day so they come for one or two courses, maybe a single glass of wine and a cup of coffee, then head out again. Our lunchtime favourites include steak sandwiches, seared fish, salads and soups – nothing too heavy that might risk sleepiness in the afternoon, though there are always those who can't resist a portion of sticky toffee pudding for dessert!

Staff lunch is at four o'clock in the afternoon, when our guests have left and the restaurant has quietened down. As a chef, you quickly get used to the strange timetable of eating meals either when most people have finished or hours before they have started. Whenever it comes, lunch is the perfect excuse to down tools.

Cooking for yourself and others can be restorative, but it needs to be relaxed and not too labour-intensive. Make soups in advance to be reheated later or prepare the components of a salad ahead so you just need to assemble it when you're ready to eat. Use up leftovers in salads and sandwiches and make double batches of recipes for twice the rewards. Many of our lunch dishes can be wrapped up for a picnic or packed into a lunch box for a welcome taste of home at work or school.

Sometimes the occasion calls for something a little bit fancier – lunch with a friend, family members coming to stay, mini celebrations – and if so you will need to up your game in the kitchen! You could perhaps make a simple but impressive tart to feed a crowd or buy some super-fresh fish and give it the Asian treatment – sear the outside and drizzle it with soy and sesame dressing.

Lunch should never be too much of a bother to put together yet worth taking a break for.

# LUNCH

Roast red pepper and tomato soup     55

Pea soup     56
*with black pudding, pea shoots and crispy shallots*

Cider and onion soup     59
*with Lincolnshire Poacher croutons*

Spiced lentil soup     60

Potted beef     63

Pan-fried English asparagus     64
*with Bayonne ham, crispy eggs and hollandaise sauce*

Steak sandwich     67

Griddled squid     68
*with chorizo and avocado salsa*

Seared salmon     71

'Nduja tuna steaks     72
*with onions and salsa verde*

Tomato and burrata tart     75

Superfood salad     76

Crispy duck salad     79

Piccalilli     80

# Roast red pepper and tomato soup

This wonderfully refreshing soup is served cold, making it ideal for a summer lunch. It needs to be made in advance so it can be cooled and chilled before serving, as this really intensifies the flavours. Serve it in chilled bowls sprinkled with diced cucumber or pour it into shot glasses for a brilliant summer canapé.

1. Preheat the oven to 200°C/180°C fan/Gas 6.

2. Put the tomatoes and peppers into separate roasting trays, drizzle with olive oil and sprinkle with salt. Roast until slightly blackened, about 40 minutes.

3. Heat the measured oil in a large saucepan, add the onion, garlic and celery, and cook gently until soft, but with no colour, about 5 minutes. Stir in the sundried tomato paste and tomato purée, and cook for 3–4 minutes, then add the roast tomatoes and peppers, bring up to a simmer and cook for 5 minutes. Pour in the hot stock and simmer for 5 minutes. Stir in the basil and cook for a couple of minutes.

4. Remove from the heat and cool slightly, then blitz until smooth, either using a stick blender in the pan or by transferring the mixture to a blender. Pass through a fine sieve into a bowl and set aside to cool, then chill in the fridge for several hours until cold.

5. Once you are ready to serve, stir in the tomato juice and season to taste with salt and pepper. Serve cold in chilled bowls and garnish each portion with some diced cucumber, a sprig of basil and a drizzle of olive oil.

SERVES 4–6

1kg plum tomatoes, halved

2 red peppers, deseeded and cut into large pieces

2 tbsp olive oil, plus extra for drizzling

1 onion, finely chopped

1 garlic clove, finely chopped

1 celery stick, trimmed and chopped

2 heaped tbsp sundried tomato paste

2 tsp tomato purée

400ml hot vegetable stock

Small handful of fresh basil leaves, plus extra to garnish

100ml tomato juice, chilled

Sea salt and freshly ground black pepper

¼ cucumber, diced, to garnish

# Pea soup

*with black pudding, pea shoots and crispy shallots*

The black pudding, pea shoots and crispy shallots that garnish this bright green soup really make it special, but you can leave out one or all of them for a simpler lunch dish. Swap the black pudding for chorizo for spicier overtones, or make the soup vegetarian by swapping the chicken stock for vegetable stock and leaving out the black pudding.

SERVES 4

30g butter

2 tbsp olive oil

4 banana shallots, 3 roughly chopped, 1 thinly sliced into rings (keep chopped and sliced separate)

100g black pudding, diced

Vegetable oil, for shallow-frying

1 tbsp cornflour

500g frozen peas

750ml chicken stock

Sea salt and freshly ground black pepper

Pea shoots, to garnish

1. Melt the butter with 1 tablespoon of the olive oil in a large saucepan, then add the chopped shallots and cook over a medium heat, stirring occasionally, until soft but not coloured, 6–8 minutes. Set aside.

2. Meanwhile, heat the remaining olive oil in a heavy-based frying pan, add the black pudding and season with pepper. Cook over a medium heat for 1–2 minutes to heat through and crisp up, stirring often. Drain on kitchen paper and set aside.

3. Pour enough vegetable oil into a small, heavy-based saucepan so it is about 1cm deep in the pan. Heat until it is very hot. Coat the sliced shallot rings in a light dusting of cornflour, separating the rings as you do so, then shallow-fry in the hot oil until golden and crisp, 4–5 minutes. Remove using a slotted spoon and drain on kitchen paper. Set aside.

4. Finish the soup. Tip the frozen peas into the pan of softened shallots, followed by the stock, and bring to the boil. Immediately remove from the heat (to keep the colour of the peas), then blitz until smooth either using a stick blender in the pan or by transferring the mixture to a blender.

5. Season to taste with salt and pepper, then pour the soup into warmed serving bowls. Garnish each portion with some black pudding, crispy shallots and pea shoots before serving.

# Cider and onion soup
## with Lincolnshire Poacher croutons

Rich and aromatic, this soup is really heartening on cold wet days. We favour grated Lincolnshire Poacher cheese melted on the sourdough croutons, but you can replace it with any mature Cheddar if you prefer. We also love the indulgent drizzle of double cream at the end, but again, you can leave it out if you like.

1. Melt the butter and oil in a large saucepan, then add the onions, garlic, thyme sprigs and bay leaf. Cook, uncovered, over a low–medium heat for 35–40 minutes, until the onions are very well reduced down and meltingly soft, but without colour. Stir often for the first 20 minutes, then occasionally for the next 15–20 minutes.

2. Pour in the cider, increase the heat a little and cook, stirring occasionally, until almost all of the liquid has disappeared, for 15–20 minutes. Stir in the chicken stock and bring to the boil, then reduce the heat and simmer for 10 minutes.

3. Meanwhile, preheat the grill to high. Lay the bread slices on a baking sheet and toast for 2 minutes on one side. Turn over and brush the top sides with a little oil, then toast again for a further 2 minutes. Scatter the grated cheese over the slices of toast, then return to the grill for a couple of minutes, until the cheese has melted.

4. Remove the soup from the heat, discard the bay leaf and thyme stalks, then stir in the cream and season to taste with salt and pepper. Blitz the soup until smooth using a stick blender in the pan or by transferring the soup to a blender.

5. Pour the soup into warmed serving bowls and place two cheesy croutons on the side of each portion. Garnish the soup with a drizzle of extra cream, if you like, then sprinkle snipped chives over the top, and serve.

SERVES 4

50g butter

1 tbsp olive oil, plus extra for brushing

1kg white or yellow onions, finely sliced

1 garlic clove, finely chopped

2 thyme sprigs

1 bay leaf

300ml dry cider

800ml chicken stock

4 slices of sourdough bread, each cut in half

100g Lincolnshire Poacher cheese or mature Cheddar cheese, grated

2 tbsp double cream, plus extra to garnish

Sea salt and freshly ground black pepper

1 tbsp finely snipped fresh chives, to garnish

# Spiced lentil soup

This soup is the perfect warming meal-in-a-bowl for winter days. Make a big batch and keep any leftovers in the fridge – it will be even better the following day as the flavours intensify and deepen. It may seem like a large quantity of vegetable stock, but all of it is required to cook the lentils as they are not pre-soaked.

1. Heat the 2 tablespoons of olive oil in a large saucepan, add the onions and garlic, and sauté over a medium heat for 6–8 minutes, until softened. Stir in the remaining 1 teaspoon of oil and all the ground spices, and cook for a couple of minutes or so, stirring, until aromatic.

2. Add the tomatoes, chilli and coriander stalks, then cook until the tomatoes start to break down, 5–6 minutes, stirring often so they don't stick. Stir in the tomato purée and cook for 1–2 minutes. Pour in the lentils and stock. Bring to the boil, then reduce the heat and simmer gently, uncovered, for 40–45 minutes, stirring occasionally, until the lentils are soft.

3. Remove from the heat, then blitz until smooth either using a stick blender in the pan or by transferring the mixture to a blender. Season to taste with salt and pepper.

4. Ladle the soup into warmed serving bowls and garnish each portion with a spoonful of yoghurt and the coriander leaves or coriander cress.

SERVES 6

2 tbsp olive oil, plus 1 tsp

250g red onions, roughly chopped

2 garlic cloves, roughly chopped

4 tsp ground cumin

½ tsp ground turmeric

1 tsp paprika

2½ tsp ground coriander

¼ tsp curry powder

500g tomatoes, quartered

1 red chilli, deseeded and roughly chopped

Small bunch of fresh coriander (about 15g), picked, stalks reserved, leaves to garnish

2 tbsp tomato purée

300g dried Puy lentils

1.75 litres vegetable stock

Sea salt and freshly ground black pepper

6 tbsp natural yoghurt, to garnish

Coriander cress, to garnish (optional)

# Potted beef

In the days before refrigeration, meats were traditionally potted to preserve them, but even though technological advances have done away with the need to cook beef this way, the results are just too delicious to allow this recipe to fall out of fashion. It makes a great addition to a picnic, cold lunch or camping expedition and goes brilliantly with the Piccalilli on page 80.

1. To cook the beef, put the brisket into a large saucepan with a lid and fill the pan with enough cold water to cover the joint. Place over a medium heat, cover and bring to the boil. As soon as the water comes to the boil, remove the pan from the heat and discard the water. There will be a lot of scum on top of the water, so skim this off first before draining the water away.

2. Fill the pan with clean cold water, again enough to cover the joint, and return to the heat. Cover with the lid. When the water starts to simmer, skim the surface of any scum and add the chopped vegetables, parsley sprigs, star anise and peppercorns. Cover again and cook over a low heat for 4 hours, until completely tender.

3. When the meat is ready, strain it, discarding the liquid and cooked vegetables. Set the beef aside to cool. When it's cool enough to handle, discard the fat around the joint, then shred the meat into small pieces while still warm. You may find this easier to do with two forks, to separate and pull the beef apart. Cool, then cover and place in the fridge until cold.

4. When you are ready to serve, measure all the ingredients for the dressing into a large bowl. Add the shredded beef and toss together well, seasoning to taste with salt and pepper.

5. Serve with Piccalilli (see page 80) and sourdough toast or crackers.

SERVES 8

*For the beef*

1kg salt beef brisket

1 carrot, peeled and roughly chopped

1 white onion, roughly chopped

1 celery stick, trimmed and roughly chopped

½ leek, trimmed and roughly chopped

6 parsley sprigs

1 star anise

5 black peppercorns

*For the potted beef dressing*

180g mayonnaise

4 tbsp Dijon mustard

4 tbsp wholegrain mustard

2 tbsp crème fraîche

Sea salt and freshly ground black pepper

*To serve*

Piccalilli (*see page 80*)

Sourdough toast or crackers

TIP

The potted beef will keep in a covered container in the fridge for up to a week.

# Pan-fried English asparagus

*with Bayonne ham, crispy eggs and hollandaise sauce*

The arrival of new-season ingredients in the kitchen is always exciting, and the beginning of the English asparagus season in May after the dreary winter months gives us a real reason to celebrate. Asparagus with hollandaise is an unbeatable pairing, but adding salty ham and crispy eggs gives even more flavour and extra texture to this old favourite.

1. Blanch the asparagus spears in a pan of boiling water for 30 seconds. Drain and immediately refresh in cold water to stop them cooking, then drain well and pat dry. Wrap two spears in a slice of Bayonne ham, repeat for all the spears. Set aside.

2. Poach the eggs in a pan of simmering water for 2½ minutes each (see Avocado and Toast with Poached Eggs on page 25 for how to poach eggs), then remove with a slotted spoon and place in a bowl of iced water to stop the eggs cooking.

3. When the eggs are cold, dry them on a clean tea towel, then roll them in the seasoned flour and dip in the egg wash. Roll them in the breadcrumbs to coat, then set aside.

4. To make the hollandaise, put the 3 egg yolks in a heatproof bowl over a pan of barely simmering water over a very low heat (the base of the bowl shouldn't touch the water). Whisk until thickened to ribbon stage (when you lift the whisk, the yolks drop and form a ribbon on the surface that holds its shape for a few minutes). Very slowly whisk in the clarified butter, until thick and smooth, then whisk in the lemon juice and salt to taste. Cover and set aside.

5. When ready to serve, heat a deep-fat fryer to 180°C or fill a large saucepan one-third full of oil and heat until a cube of bread dropped in the oil sizzles and turns golden in 30 seconds. Fry the eggs for about 2 minutes, until golden brown all over, then remove with a slotted spoon and drain on kitchen paper.

6. Meanwhile, heat the olive oil in a frying pan over a medium heat until hot, add the ham-wrapped asparagus spears and pan-fry for 3–5 minutes, turning occasionally, until the ham starts to crisp.

7. Divide the asparagus among two plates and spoon over a dollop of hollandaise. Place a crispy egg on top of the hollandaise and sprinkle with grated Parmesan before serving.

SERVES 2

12 asparagus spears

6 slices of Bayonne ham

2 duck or hen eggs

30g plain flour (seasoned with salt and pepper), for dusting

1 egg yolk, beaten with a splash of milk (for the egg wash)

50g panko breadcrumbs or ordinary breadcrumbs

3 egg yolks

250g clarified butter, melted (*see Béarnaise sauce page 125 for how to make clarified butter*)

Juice of ½ lemon

Sea salt

Vegetable oil, for deep-frying

1½ tsp olive oil

25g Parmesan cheese, grated, to serve

TIP
Keep any leftover hollandaise sauce in a covered bowl in the fridge for up to 2 days. Warm through gently (in a heatproof bowl set over a pan of barely simmering water over a very low heat), before serving.

# Steak sandwich

Nothing beats a good steak sandwich for a weekend lunch and we think this is a particularly good one. You don't have to add the truffle oil to the dressing, but it changes this from a great steak sandwich to a superlative one. You can use leftover cooked steak if you prefer, and swap the sourdough toast for baguette or thick slices of crusty white bread.

1. Melt the butter with the measured vegetable oil in a saucepan, add the onion and cook over a low heat, stirring regularly, until very soft and caramelised – this will take about 10 minutes. Season with a little salt and pepper. Set aside.

2. Meanwhile, heat a heavy-based frying pan over a high heat until smoking hot. Rub the surface of the steak with vegetable oil and place it in the pan. Cook for 2–3 minutes on each side for a medium–rare steak, longer if you prefer it well done. Remove the steak from the pan and leave to rest for at least 5 minutes.

3. While the meat is resting, make the dressing. Mix the mayonnaise, mustard, horseradish and oil (if using) together in a small bowl.

4. Toast the bread slices in a toaster or under a preheated grill, or brush them with vegetable oil and cook them briefly on a very hot griddle pan to create distinctive charred lines.

5. Dress the watercress or rocket with a little olive oil. Finely slice the rested beef and season with salt and pepper.

6. Spread the toast with some of the dressing (see Tip) and then divide the steak among two of the toasted bread slices. Spoon the caramelised onions on top, followed by some watercress or rocket. Finally, put the remaining two slices of toast on top, slice the sandwich in half and serve immediately.

SERVES 2

15g butter

1½ tsp vegetable oil, plus extra for the steak and toast

1 onion, finely sliced

1 thick-cut sirloin steak, about 250g

4 slices of sourdough bread

2 small handfuls of watercress or rocket

Extra virgin olive oil, for drizzling

Sea salt and freshly ground black pepper

*For the dressing*

4 tbsp mayonnaise

2 tbsp wholegrain mustard

1 tbsp creamed horseradish

2 tsp truffle oil or olive oil (optional)

TIP

Any leftover dressing will keep in a covered bowl in the fridge for a couple of days.

# Griddled squid

*with chorizo and avocado salsa*

Marinating the squid with kiwi fruit may seem strange, but the fruit contains an enzyme called actinidin, which breaks down protein and tenderises the potentially tough flesh of the squid, making it softer to eat. Remember to rinse the squid afterwards, though, and dry it thoroughly so it chars properly on the griddle.

1. Put the butterflied squid and tentacles into a bowl with the kiwi slices and mix together with your hands. Transfer to the fridge and leave to soften for 30–60 minutes.

2. Put the red onion, red pepper, avocado, half of the lime zest, the lime juice, chopped mint and chilli sauce into a separate bowl, and mix together. Season with salt and pepper, and set aside.

3. Meanwhile, put the chorizo into a small frying pan and place over a medium heat (there's no need to add oil). Cook for 2–3 minutes, stirring regularly, until the chorizo is golden. Set aside.

4. Remove the squid from the kiwi, discarding the fruit. Rinse the squid and pat dry with kitchen paper. Heat a griddle pan over a high heat until very hot. Rub the squid all over with a dash of vegetable oil, then add to the hot pan and cook for about 1 minute on each side, until the squid turns opaque, starts to curl up and is tender.

5. Divide the squid among four serving plates, then top with the avocado salsa. Spoon some of the chorizo onto each plate, then finish each with a small handful of rocket. Drizzle with the chorizo oil from the pan and then sprinkle with the remaining lime zest before serving.

SERVES 4

4 squid (about 400g), cleaned and butterflied, with tentacles intact (see Tip)

1 kiwi, peeled and sliced

1 small red onion, diced

1 small red pepper, deseeded and diced

1 small ripe avocado, peeled, stoned and diced

Finely grated zest and juice of 2 limes

2 mint sprigs, leaves picked and chopped

3 tbsp sweet chilli sauce

100g cooking chorizo, chopped

Dash of vegetable oil (about 1 tsp)

4 small handfuls of rocket

Sea salt and freshly ground black pepper

TIP

If using squid with the tentacles intact, trim off the straggly ends and beaks first.

# Seared salmon

You need to use the freshest salmon possible for this recipe, as the fish is served raw in the middle. Buy the salmon from a fishmonger you trust and always use it on the day of purchase. The delicious dressing is excellent and can also be used as a dipping sauce for cooked prawns, crispy squid or chargrilled chicken skewers.

1. Toast the sesame seeds in a small, dry frying pan over a medium heat for a few minutes, keeping a careful eye on them so they don't burn. Shake the pan from time to time. Tip into a small bowl and set aside.

2. Rub the salmon fillet all over with a little vegetable oil and season with salt. Heat a heavy-based frying pan over a high heat until hot, then sear the salmon fillet for 1 minute on each side. Transfer the salmon to a plate and leave to cool, then coat with the toasted sesame seeds.

3. To make the dressing, put the onion, garlic, ginger and rice vinegar into a blender, and blitz together until smooth. Add all the remaining ingredients and blend again until thoroughly combined.

4. Slice the salmon into 5mm slices and lay on four serving plates. Drizzle the salmon with plenty of dressing (see Tip) and garnish with the diced avocado and coriander leaves. Serve with sushi rice, steamed Tenderstem broccoli and spinach or bok choy.

SERVES 4

10g mixed black and white sesame seeds

500g single piece of salmon fillet, skin removed

Vegetable oil, for cooking

Sea salt

1 avocado, peeled, stoned and diced, to garnish

Handful of fresh coriander leaves, to garnish

Sushi rice, steamed Tenderstem broccoli and spinach or bok choy, to serve

*For the dressing*

½ white onion, roughly chopped

1 small garlic clove, peeled

2cm piece of fresh root ginger (about 10g), peeled and sliced

2 tbsp rice vinegar

4 tbsp soy sauce

55ml vegetable oil

1 tbsp sesame oil

1 tsp chilli oil, or more to taste

30g caster sugar

1 tsp English mustard

TIP
Keep any leftover dressing in a screw-top jar in the fridge for up to a week.

# 'Nduja tuna steaks

*with onions and salsa verde*

The combination of flavours in this dish is incredible and it's great for a Valentine's Day or special birthday lunch. 'Nduja is a spreadable spicy pork salami from the Calabria region of Italy, which melts beautifully on the tuna steaks when heated in the griddle pan. Please note, though, that 'nduja is a pretty fiery ingredient, so this is definitely one for chilli lovers.

1. To make the salsa verde, put all the ingredients into a blender and pulse a few times until roughly chopped and well combined, adding enough olive oil to loosen the mixture to your preferred consistency. Season well with salt and pepper. If the salsa is very thick, you can stir in 1 tablespoon of cold water to loosen. Cover and set aside.

2. To cook the onions, heat a griddle pan over a medium–high heat until it is really hot. Drizzle some olive oil over the onions, then season with salt and pepper. Place the onions into the hot pan and cook for 5–6 minutes, turning occasionally, until they are nicely charred. Divide the onions among two warmed serving plates and set aside.

3. Season the tuna steaks, then place them in the hot pan and sear for 1 minute on each side. Carefully spread the 'nduja on one side (the side facing upwards) of each tuna steak, then turn each one over so the 'nduja side is now facing down in the pan and cook for 30 seconds. Carefully lift each tuna steak from the griddle pan using a fish slice to make sure the 'nduja stays on the fish.

4. Place the seared tuna steaks on top of the charred onions, 'nduja side up. Drizzle each portion with some salsa verde, then serve immediately.

SERVES 2

Olive oil, for drizzling

150–200g calçot or grelot onions, peeled, cleaned and halved lengthways (see Tip)

2 tuna steaks, about 150–175g each, cut from the thinner end of the tuna fillet

50g 'nduja (Italian spicy spreadable pork salami)

*For the salsa verde* (see Tip)

25g cornichons, drained weight

35g small capers, drained weight

1½ tsp Dijon mustard

3 tinned anchovy fillets, drained

Small bunch of fresh flat leaf parsley (about 25g)

Small bunch of fresh basil (about 25g)

Small handful of fresh mint (about 10g)

1 tbsp red wine vinegar, or to taste

4–5 tbsp extra virgin olive oil, to loosen

Sea salt and freshly ground black pepper

TIPS
Calçot onions are large, mild spring onions from Catalonia in Spain, available February to March. You can use French grelot onions, large, fat spring onions or baby leeks, if in season.
  Store any leftover salsa in a screw-top jar or covered bowl in the fridge for up to 5 days.

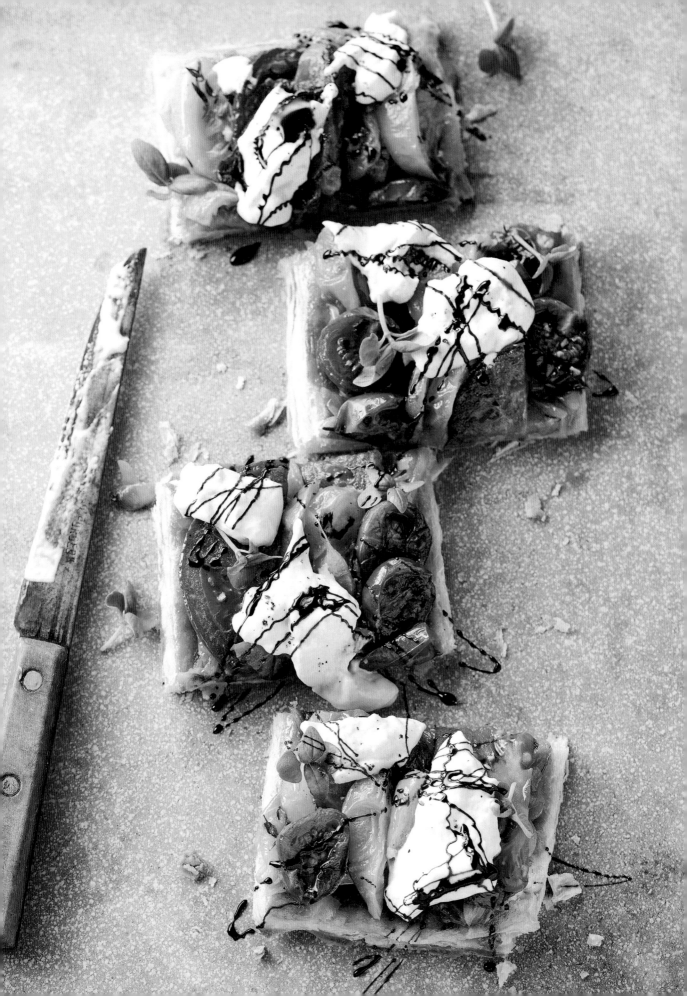

# Tomato and burrata tart

It is not absolutely essential to marinate the tomatoes in the spices, but it does give this tart a lovely flavour and a great kick. As with all recipes that use fresh tomatoes, adding a pinch of caster sugar will bring out the sweetness in the fruit, especially when the tomatoes aren't quite as ripe as you'd like. Serve this impressive savoury tart at a high-summer lunch party with a big green salad. It will taste as stunning as it looks.

1. Put all the ingredients for the marinade into a blender and blitz to chop the garlic and red chilli more finely. Set aside.

2. Heat the oil in a large pan, add the onions and 5 tablespoons of water, and season with salt. Cover with a lid and place over a high heat for a couple of minutes. Once the onions are sizzling, reduce the heat right down and cook for 15 minutes, stirring occasionally, until they have softened. Take the lid off the pan and increase the heat slightly. Add the butter and cook for about 15 minutes, stirring regularly, until the onions have caramelised. Set aside.

3. Meanwhile, cut each large heritage tomato in half, then cut each half into four wedges. Put into a bowl with the cherry tomatoes, if using, and red onion. Pour over the marinade, and toss the tomatoes and onions until well coated. Season with a generous pinch of salt and the sugar, then set aside for 30–45 minutes until the juices are released from the tomatoes.

4. Preheat the oven to 200°C/180°C fan/Gas 6.

5. Unroll the puff pastry onto a lightly floured surface and trim the edges to make a large rectangle measuring 32 x 24cm. Prick all over with a fork, then transfer the pastry to a baking sheet. Bake in the oven for 10–12 minutes, turning the baking sheet around halfway through, until the pastry is puffed up and pale golden.

6. Remove from the oven and spoon the caramelised onions evenly over the pastry base, leaving a 1cm border all around the edge. Return to the oven and bake for a further 6 minutes.

7. Remove from the oven again and use a slotted spoon to place the marinated tomatoes on top of the onions. Discard the juices (see Tip). Return to the oven and bake for a further 15–20 minutes, until the tomatoes and onions are cooked, and the pastry is deep golden and crisp.

8. Top the baked tart with the burrata and a sprinkling of basil leaves. Finish with a drizzle of balsamic glaze and serve sliced.

MAKES 1 LARGE TART/
SERVES 6-8

*For the marinade*

½ tsp ground cumin

½ tsp ground coriander

½–1 red chilli, deseeded
  and chopped

1 garlic clove, chopped

50ml olive oil


*For the tart*

5 tbsp olive oil

5 white onions, finely sliced

Sea salt

30g butter

5 large heritage tomatoes

Handful of cherry tomatoes,
  halved (optional)

1 small red onion, finely sliced

Generous pinch of caster sugar

500g ready-rolled all-butter
  puff pastry

Plain flour, for dusting

1 burrata, sliced or torn into
  pieces and seasoned with salt

1 tbsp small basil leaves

Good-quality aged balsamic
  vinegar glaze, to finish


TIP
Use the leftover marinade from the tomatoes and onions to marinate raw peeled prawns or chicken breast fillets (sliced into strips) to add flavour to them before stir-frying.

# Superfood salad

All the ingredients in this super healthy salad are good for you. This might make it sound a bit worthy, but the combination of colours, textures and flavours is an absolute knockout. Serve it to a large group of friends or make a big batch for packed lunches to take to work. It also works brilliantly as a side dish for grilled fish or chicken. Add a couple of handfuls of raw kale if you want to feel even more virtuous.

1. Preheat the oven to 240°C/220°C fan/Gas 9.

2. Toss the butternut squash pieces in the olive oil until coated, then lay them out on a baking tray. Roast for 20 minutes, until tender, then leave to cool.

3. Toast the pumpkin or hemp seeds in a small, dry frying pan over a medium heat for a few minutes, shaking the pan occasionally. Tip into a small bowl and set aside.

4. Meanwhile, blanch the Tenderstem broccoli and broccoli florets in a large pan of boiling water for 1 minute, then remove with a slotted spoon and drain well. Blanch the soy beans in the same pan for 1 minute, then drain well and set aside.

5. Heat a griddle pan over a high heat until very hot, then griddle both types of broccoli for 1–2 minutes, turning occasionally. (Depending on the pan you use, you may need to lightly brush the broccoli with a little vegetable oil before griddling.)

6. Put the squash, pumpkin or hemp seeds, both types of broccoli, the soy beans and all the remaining ingredients, except the yoghurt and lemon juice, in a large bowl and toss together to mix.

7. Mix the yoghurt and lemon juice together in a small bowl, season with salt and pepper, then stir through the salad. Divide the salad among individual plates and serve.

SERVES 6–8

1 small butternut squash (about 500g), peeled, deseeded and cut into small wedges or half moons

2 tbsp olive oil

2 tbsp pumpkin or hemp seeds

200g Tenderstem broccoli

200g broccoli florets

80g young soy beans (you need about 200g edamame pods), or use frozen

Vegetable oil, for brushing

120g mixed salad leaves

90g red cabbage (about 2cm wedge), shredded

1 cos lettuce, shredded

60g cooked cold quinoa (see Tip)

Small handful of fresh mint leaves, chopped

Small handful of fresh flat leaf parsley leaves, chopped

50g alfalfa sprouts

3 tbsp natural yoghurt

Juice of 1 lemon

Sea salt and freshly ground black pepper

TIP
Cook the quinoa in hot vegetable stock until tender, according to the packet instructions. Drain and set aside to cool.

# Crispy duck salad

Cooking the duck for this Asian-style salad may take a while, but it involves virtually no effort and you can spend the time calmly preparing the other ingredients and making the dressing. Once the duck is cooked and shredded, it's then a simple assembly job. The combination of the crispy duck with the crunchy radish, peppery watercress, hot dressing and fresh coriander is sensational.

1. Preheat the oven to 190°C/170°C fan/Gas 5.

2. Place the duck legs on a baking tray, season with salt, then cook in the oven for 2 hours until tender and crispy.

3. While the duck legs are cooking, make the dressing. Put the ginger into a bottle or jar with the lemongrass and chilli halves. Pour the lime and lemon juices into the bottle, add the soy sauce and olive oil, season with salt and pepper, then put the lid on and shake the bottle well. Leave to infuse until you are ready to serve. Strain before using.

4. When the duck legs are completely crispy, remove from the oven and leave to cool. Once they are cool enough to handle, pick the meat from the bones, discarding any soft fat. Use two forks to do this – the meat should come away from the bones very easily. Place the picked meat in a bowl.

5. Mix the orange juice, tomato ketchup, honey, soy sauce and sesame oil together in a bowl. Add this sauce to the shredded duck and stir through until well mixed.

6. Combine the watercress, chillies, ginger, mooli/daikon and radishes in a separate large serving bowl, add the salad dressing (minus the aromatics) and toss to mix. Add half of the coriander leaves, spring onions and toasted sesame seeds, and toss to mix.

7. Serve the salad on a platter or individual plates with the crispy duck on top, then sprinkle with the remaining coriander, spring onions and sesame seeds.

SERVES 4

4 duck legs

Juice of 1 large orange

160g tomato ketchup

40g runny honey

40ml soy sauce

40ml sesame oil

100g watercress

½–1 red chilli, deseeded and cut into julienne

½–1 green chilli, deseeded and cut into julienne

Thumb-sized piece of fresh root ginger, peeled and cut into julienne

⅓ mooli/daikon (Japanese radish), cut into julienne

10 radishes, sliced

Large handful of fresh coriander, leaves picked

Bunch of spring onions, trimmed and sliced

2 tbsp mixed black and white sesame seeds, toasted (see Seared Salmon on page 71 for how to toast sesame seeds)

Sea salt and freshly ground black pepper

*For the dressing*

Thumb-sized piece of fresh root ginger, peeled

1 lemongrass stalk, cut in half

1 red chilli, cut in half

Juice of 1 lime

Juice of 1 lemon

1 tbsp dark soy sauce

3 tbsp extra virgin olive oil

# Piccalilli

Home-made piccalilli is a completely different animal to the glow-in-the-dark, vinegary condiment you can buy. It is zingy and fresh-tasting with just-cooked vegetables and a nice amount of heat. It is an excellent accompaniment to the Potted beef on page 63, as well as other cold meats, cheeses and pork pies.

1. Put the cauliflower florets into a colander and sprinkle with the salt. Set aside at room temperature for at least 5 hours. Rinse well under cold running water, then drain.

2. Pour the vinegar into a saucepan and bring to the boil, then let it bubble and reduce for 5 minutes. Measure the sugar, turmeric and mustard powder into a large bowl. Slowly pour in the vinegar reduction, stirring constantly, until combined. Return the mixture to the pan.

3. Blend the cornflour with 4–5 tablespoons of cold water in a small bowl, until smooth, then stir this into the vinegar base, mixing it well. Add the cauliflower florets and cook for 5 minutes, stirring every now and then so that the cornflour cooks evenly through the sauce. Stir in the onions and cook for a further 5 minutes, continuing to stir well as before. Add the gherkins, then remove from the heat. Taste and add a little more salt, if required.

4. Spoon the piccalilli into hot, sterilised jars (see Tip). Seal with vinegar-proof lids and leave to cool. Serve once cold, or store in a cool, dark place for up to a month before opening. Once opened, store in the fridge for up to a week.

MAKES ABOUT 4 X 400G JARS

500g cauliflower florets
   (about 1 small cauliflower)

2–3 tbsp table salt

560ml white wine vinegar

215g caster sugar

1 tbsp ground turmeric

80g English mustard powder

50g cornflour

200g baby onions, peeled
   and halved if large

160g gherkins, drained weight,
   diced

TIP
To sterilise jars, and their lids, wash them thoroughly and leave to dry on a clean tea towel. Preheat the oven to its lowest setting, then place the jars and lids on a baking tray and heat in the oven for 30 minutes.

# FOOD FOR SHARING

We host a lot of parties at Bread Street, from ten mates gathering for a friend's birthday to 200 guests at a wedding. Whether they are sitting down for a meal or standing up at a reception, everybody loves our sharing platters of sticky chicken wings, salt and pepper squid and famous flatbreads from the wood oven. It's such a sociable way to eat and everybody gets to try lots of different dishes. Also, doesn't everything somehow taste better when you eat it with your hands?

This sort of food – savoury, moreish, finger-lickingly good – is perfect for feeding a crowd at informal gatherings, such as watching a match with friends or movie night with the family. Make a selection of flatbreads for a teenage sleepover, kick off an al fresco lunch with some home-made grissini and dips, or take venison Scotch eggs to a picnic. A freshly baked focaccia served with some good-quality olive oil and balsamic vinegar makes a simple but popular accompaniment to a round of beers, and a bowl of piquant spiced prawns put in the centre of the table is a great ice-breaker at a dinner party.

It isn't hard to make these sharing dishes and much of the preparation can be done in advance, leaving you with just a bit of last-minute cooking and plating up. If you're feeding a crowd, you can double the quantities for larger groups or serve two or three dishes at the same time, though this will obviously mean spending more time in the kitchen. Use big platters, bowls or chopping boards for serving and don't forget a finger bowl for sticky fingers. Then stand back and expect to watch the food you have lovingly prepared disappear in minutes.

# FOOD FOR SHARING

# Broad bean, spinach and mint dip

This vibrant green dip makes a change from houmous or guacamole. Broad beans are only in season in June, July and August, so serve a big bowlful of this dip for guests to nibble on before a summer lunch, or as part of a picnic. Only the tender, bright green beans are used, so double-podding, although a bit boring, is essential to get rid of the tough outer grey skins.

1. Bring a pan of water to the boil, then add the broad beans, bring back to the boil and cook for about 3 minutes until tender. Remove from the heat and tip the beans into a colander, then place under running cold water to cool them quickly. When they are cool enough to handle, pop the bright green beans out of their grey skins by squeezing them gently. Set aside.

2. Put the spinach into a large heatproof bowl. Pour over boiling water to cover and leave for 30 seconds, just until wilted. Drain immediately and cool quickly under running cold water. Squeeze out any excess water, then pat dry on kitchen paper and roughly chop the spinach.

3. Place the skinned beans in a blender with the spinach, mint and butter, and blitz together until thoroughly combined. Season to taste with salt and pepper.

4. Scrape into a serving bowl and serve with Poppy seed grissini (see page 90), or toasted crusty bread and crudités.

SERVES 4–6

500g fresh broad beans, podded weight (you need about 1.75–2kg broad beans in their pods)

150g spinach, rinsed

4 tbsp chopped fresh mint

50g butter, softened

Sea salt and freshly ground black pepper

Toasted crusty bread and crudités, to serve

# Poppy seed grissini

Grissini are thin, crisp breadsticks made by rolling strips of dough into long pencils and baking them in the oven. It is important that the water is the right temperature because if it is too cold, the yeast won't work its magic, and if it is too hot it will be killed off. You can replace the poppy seeds with sesame, nigella, caraway or onion seeds or use a pinch of dried chilli flakes for a little kick.

1. Put the flour into a mixing bowl. Pour the salt onto one side of the flour and the yeast onto another. Cover each with a bit of flour. Make a well in the middle of the flour and pour in the warm water, oil and malt extract or honey. Stir everything together with a table knife until the mixture forms a craggy dough, then knead with your hands to bring all the ingredients together. Transfer to a clean work surface and knead well for 5–8 minutes until the dough is soft and sticky.

2. Put the dough into an oiled clean bowl, cover with cling film and leave to rise in a warm place for 20–30 minutes, until the dough has puffed up slightly.

3. Preheat the oven to 170°C/150°C fan/Gas 3. Line a large baking sheet with baking parchment.

4. Pull off small pieces of dough, about 10g each. Oil your hands lightly and roll each piece into a long, thin stick about 24cm in length, then sprinkle a few poppy seeds over the top. Transfer to the prepared baking sheet. Continue in the same way until you've shaped and sprinkled all the dough.

5. Bake for 20–25 minutes, until golden brown and crisp, turning over halfway through baking. Transfer the grissini to a wire rack and leave to cool before serving. Store in an airtight container for up to 5 days.

MAKES ABOUT 20
GRISSINI/BREADSTICKS

125g strong white bread flour

½ tsp sea salt

½ tsp fast-action dried yeast

75ml warm water (made by mixing 50ml cold and 25ml boiling water)

1 tsp olive oil, plus extra for greasing and rolling out

¼ tsp malt extract or runny honey

1 tbsp poppy seeds

TIP
Try wrapping the grissini with Parma ham just before serving.

# Salt and pepper squid

This is a hugely popular bar snack at Bread Street Kitchen and is brilliant for sharing with friends over a cold drink. The ground Szechuan peppercorns in the coating give the crispy squid its distinct flavour and mouth-numbing tingle, but leave them out if you aren't a fan, or use black peppercorns instead.

SERVES 4–6

2½ tsp Szechuan peppercorns

50g plain flour

50g cornflour

50g semolina

¾ tsp sea salt

Vegetable oil, for deep-frying

12 small squid (about 550g), cleaned, patted dry and sliced into rings

120ml whole milk

*To serve*

1 plump red chilli, deseeded and finely sliced

Large handful of fresh coriander leaves

Lime wedges

1. Toast the peppercorns in a dry frying pan over a medium–high heat for a few minutes, shaking the pan occasionally. Remove from the heat and blitz them to a fine powder in a spice grinder or crush them using a pestle and mortar. Mix 2 teaspoons of the ground peppercorns (reserve the rest for sprinkling later) with the flour, cornflour, semolina and salt in a bowl. Set aside on a large plate.

2. Heat a deep-fat fryer to 180°C or fill a large saucepan one-third full of vegetable oil and heat until a cube of bread dropped in the oil sizzles and turns golden in 30 seconds.

3. Put the squid into a separate bowl and pour over the milk, then remove the squid rings in batches, shaking off the excess milk, and immediately dip in the flour mixture to coat all over, shaking off the excess flour, too.

4. Deep-fry the squid rings in batches in the hot oil for 2–3 minutes per batch, until golden brown all over, turning them over occasionally if necessary so they brown evenly. Remove with a slotted spoon, drain on kitchen paper, then keep warm in a low oven while you deep-fry the remaining squid rings in the same way, making sure you bring the oil back up to temperature between each batch.

5. Transfer the deep-fried squid rings to serving plates, scatter with the chilli slices and coriander leaves, then garnish with lime wedges. Serve immediately, sprinkling a little of the reserved pepper over each serving, to taste.

# Spiced prawns

These tasty prawns are perfect for a summer barbecue with friends. They take a long time to marinate but only a few minutes to cook, making them a brilliant prepare-ahead dish for entertaining. Expect much lip-smacking and finger-licking as your friends try to catch every last drop of the delicious sauce.

1. Mix the ground spices together, then place in a dry frying pan over a low heat. Toast the spices gently for 5 minutes, shaking the pan from time to time. Stir in 25ml of the olive oil and cook gently for 5 minutes. Leave to cool.

2. Put the onion, garlic, lemon juice, chopped herbs and toasted spice mixture into a mixing bowl. Add half of the remaining olive oil and blitz with a stick blender to a thick paste. Add the remaining olive oil, season with salt and pepper, and blitz briefly to mix. Add the raw prawns to the marinade, turning to coat them all over. Cover and leave to marinate in the fridge for 2 hours.

3. Remove the prawns from the fridge 15 minutes before cooking to allow them to come to room temperature.

4. Heat a large griddle or frying pan or a barbecue until very hot, then cook the prawns in batches (about five at a time) for 2 minutes on each side.

5. Transfer the prawns to a serving platter, garnish with lime quarters and serve with a crunchy salad and crusty bread for mopping up the juices.

SERVES 4

2 tsp ground cumin

2 tsp ground coriander

1 tsp ground turmeric

1½ tsp sweet paprika

1 tsp smoked paprika

1 tsp cayenne pepper

100ml olive oil

1 small red onion,
    roughly chopped

1 garlic clove,
    roughly chopped

Juice of 1 lemon

3 coriander sprigs,
    roughly chopped

3 flat leaf parsley sprigs,
    roughly chopped

500g raw large prawns

Sea salt and freshly ground
    black pepper

Lime quarters, to garnish

Crunchy salad and crusty bread,
    to serve

# Flatbreads

At Bread Street, we have a wood oven that is perfect for cooking pizzas and flatbreads at a high temperature, but you can easily cook them at home in a very hot oven. Once you have made a batch of dough, you can get creative with the toppings. To get you started, on pages 97 and 98 you'll find two popular versions that are almost always on the restaurant menu.

1. Put the flour into a mixing bowl, then sprinkle the yeast on one side and the salt on the other. Cover each with a little flour. Make a well in the middle and add the warm water and oil. Mix well with a table knife to make a craggy dough, then transfer to a clean work surface and knead until smooth. This will take 8–10 minutes. (You can make the dough using a stand mixer fitted with a dough hook, if you prefer.)

2. Brush the surface of the dough with a little olive oil and place in an oiled clean bowl. Cover with cling film and leave to rise at (warm) room temperature for 45 minutes, until puffed up a little and almost doubled in size.

3. Meanwhile, prepare one of the toppings – see pages 97 and 98.

4. Preheat the oven to 220°C/200°C fan/Gas 7. Grease a large baking tray and set aside.

5. Divide the dough into four equal pieces. Shape each piece into a ball and roll out on a lightly floured surface to a rectangle or 16cm circle, 3–5mm thick. Prick the flatbreads all over with a fork, then transfer to the prepared baking tray and bake for 2 minutes (do not allow them to colour).

6. Remove from the oven, top with your chosen topping and continue as the topping recipe directs on pages 97 and 98.

SERVES 4

200g strong white bread flour, plus extra for dusting

½ tsp fast-action dried yeast

1 tsp sea salt

125ml lukewarm water

1 tsp extra virgin olive oil, plus extra for brushing

# Caramelised onion, pesto and Taleggio flatbreads

1. Heat the olive oil in a saucepan over a medium heat, then add the onions and 3 tablespoons of water. Season with salt and pepper. Cover the pan with a lid and cook over a high heat for a couple of minutes until the onions have started to soften. Reduce the heat to low and continue to cook the onions for 30 minutes, stirring regularly to prevent any catching on the pan. Remove the lid and increase the heat, then cook for a further 5 minutes, stirring well, until the onions start to caramelise and turn golden.

2. Meanwhile, toast the pine nuts in a dry frying pan over a medium heat for a couple of minutes, until golden, shaking the pan from time to time to stop them burning.

3. Preheat the oven to 220°C/200°C fan/Gas 7.

4. Divide the caramelised onions among the four flatbreads and spread evenly. Lay the Taleggio slices on top. Bake for about 12 minutes or until the cheese is melting.

5. Drizzle each flatbread with ½ tablespoon of the pesto and scatter with the toasted pine nuts, then slice the flatbreads with a pizza wheel or sharp knife to serve.

MAKES ENOUGH TO TOP 4 FLATBREADS (*see opposite*)

3 tbsp olive oil

3 large onions, finely sliced

20g pine nuts

150g Taleggio cheese, sliced

2 tbsp fresh pesto

Sea salt and freshly ground black pepper

TIP

For an optional extra, cook 6 slices of Parma ham in a hot frying pan for a couple of minutes or so, until crisp. Break into shards and scatter over the flatbreads just before serving for added crunch.

# Butternut squash, mushroom and Gruyère flatbreads

1. Preheat the oven to 220°C/200°C fan/Gas 7.

2. Put the butternut squash into a bowl, pour over 1 tablespoon of the oil and toss to coat well. Spread out the squash on a baking tray and season with salt and pepper. Roast for 18–20 minutes, until the squash is tender, then mash with a fork and leave to cool.

3. Mix the mushrooms, remaining oil and the thyme together, and season well. Spread out on a separate baking tray and roast (at the same time as the squash, if you like) for 10 minutes, until golden and tender.

4. Fry the kale in 2–3cm of oil for 2–3 minutes until crisp then drain well on kitchen paper and set aside.

5. Divide the mashed squash among the flatbreads and spread evenly, then add a layer of mushrooms on top. Lay the cheese slices on top.

6. Bake for about 12 minutes or until the cheese has melted. Scatter with the olives, toasted pine nuts and the fried kale, finish with a pinch of salt, then slice the flatbreads with a pizza wheel or a sharp knife to serve.

MAKES ENOUGH TO TOP 4 FLATBREADS (*see page 96*)

½ butternut squash (about 320g unpeeled), peeled, deseeded and chopped

2 tbsp olive oil

200g flat mushrooms (or use chestnut mushrooms), sliced

2 thyme sprigs, leaves picked

2 handfuls of curly kale, roughly chopped

150g Gruyère cheese, sliced

8–10 large green olives, pitted and quartered

2 tbsp toasted pine nuts

Sea salt and freshly ground black pepper

# Rosemary and Parmesan focaccia

Focaccia is a really easy bread to make at home and this one, topped with rosemary sprigs and melted cheese, looks really impressive and tastes so good. Serve it with some good-quality extra virgin olive oil and aged balsamic vinegar to dip into. Other ingredients that work well scattered on top are thyme sprigs, finely sliced onions (red or white), black olives and roasted garlic.

1. Put the flour into a mixing bowl, then sprinkle the yeast on one side and the measured salt on the other. Cover each with a little flour. Make a well in the middle and add the warm water and oil. Mix well with a table knife to make a softish dough (you may need to add another tablespoon of warm water), then transfer to a clean work surface and knead until smooth. This will take 8–10 minutes. (You can make the dough using a stand mixer fitted with a dough hook, if you prefer.)

2. Brush the surface of the dough with a little olive oil and place in an oiled clean bowl. Cover with cling film and leave to rise in a warm place until doubled in size, at least 1 hour.

3. Grease a large baking tray, about 35 x 28cm. Scoop the dough out of the bowl and place onto the preparing baking tray, then flatten the dough a little to shape into a rectangle and spray or brush lightly with more oil. Cover with cling film, as before, and leave in a warm place for 30 minutes or until doubled in size.

4. Preheat the oven to 200°C/180°C fan/Gas 6.

5. Using your fingers, press vigorously all over the surface of the dough to knock it back and create air pockets. The dough should now be about 28 x 23cm in size. Sprinkle with the grated cheese, rosemary leaves and some sea salt flakes. Drizzle with a little more olive oil for a nice colour.

6. Bake for 20–25 minutes, until golden and cooked through. Transfer to a wire rack and leave to cool slightly, then slice and serve warm. Once baked, you can drizzle the top of the focaccia with a little more oil, if you like.

SERVES 6-8

375g strong white bread flour

1 x 7g sachet fast-action dried yeast

1½ tsp sea salt

About 225ml lukewarm water

40ml olive oil, plus extra for brushing and drizzling

50g Parmesan or pecorino cheese, grated

3 rosemary sprigs, leaves picked

Sea salt flakes

# Tamarind-spiced chicken wings

This is an iconic Bread Street Kitchen dish, which, despite the slightly daunting number of ingredients, isn't complicated to cook at home. The key to the sweet-and-sour sauce is the tamarind, which can easily be found in Asian supermarkets or bought online; it adds a distinctive tang to the sauce that is completely delicious.

1. For the marinade, beat the egg in a large bowl, mix in the spices, mustard and oil and add the chicken wings, stirring to coat. Cover with cling film and place in the fridge for 1 hour, or ideally overnight.

2. For the tamarind sauce, place a dry frying pan over a medium heat and when it's hot, add the chilli flakes and all the seeds and heat for 1–2 minutes to release the aromas. Remove from the heat and crush to a coarse powder using a pestle and mortar or spice grinder. Set aside.

3. Heat the oil in a large saucepan over a medium heat, then add the onion and cook, stirring occasionally, until soft, 6–8 minutes. Stir in the crushed spices and cook for 2 minutes, stirring often, then stir in the tomato purée and cook for a further 1–2 minutes, stirring. Add the sugar, honey, tomato ketchup, Worcestershire sauce, vinegar, tamarind paste and chicken stock and stir to combine. Bring to the boil, then reduce the heat, cover and simmer, uncovered, for 55 minutes–1 hour, until the sauce has reduced slightly and is infused with all the spices.

4. Pass the sauce through a fine sieve set over a clean saucepan, pressing it with a wooden spoon. Discard the onion pulp. Bring to the boil, then reduce the heat to medium and let it bubble, uncovered, for 30–35 minutes, until the sauce has reduced and thickened and coats the back of a spoon. It will look like a thick, rich, glossy gravy. Season with salt, if needed, and keep warm.

5. Remove the marinated chicken from the fridge. Season the flour with salt, put on a large plate and lightly coat each wing in the flour.

6. Heat a deep-fat fryer to 180°C or fill a large saucepan one-third full of oil and heat until a cube of bread dropped in the oil sizzles and turns golden in 30 seconds. Deep-fry the wings (in 2–3 batches) in the oil over a medium–high heat for about 10 minutes, until cooked through and golden all over, turning occasionally if necessary. Remove with a slotted spoon and drain on kitchen paper. Keep warm in a low oven while you cook the rest, bringing the oil back up to temperature.

7. Once all the chicken wings are cooked, coat them in some of the warm tamarind sauce, then pile them onto a serving platter. Garnish with the spring onions and chopped coriander and serve with the remaining sauce. Remember to hand out lots of paper napkins!

SERVES 6-8

1kg chicken wings, rinsed and patted dry
80g plain flour
Vegetable oil, for deep-frying

*For the marinade*
1 large egg
2 tsp paprika
1 tsp ground cumin
½ tsp ground coriander
½ tsp garam masala
½ tsp Dijon mustard
1 tsp vegetable oil

*For the tamarind sauce*
1 tsp dried chilli flakes
2 tsp fennel or caraway seeds
2 tsp cumin seeds
2 tsp coriander seeds
2 tbsp vegetable oil
1 large white onion, sliced
2 tbsp tomato purée
50g light soft brown sugar
75g runny honey
4 tbsp tomato ketchup
5 tbsp Worcestershire sauce
4 tbsp white wine vinegar
3 tbsp tamarind paste (from a jar)
1 litre good-quality chicken stock
Sea salt

*To garnish*
4 spring onions, trimmed and thinly sliced on the diagonal
Torn fresh coriander leaves

# Venison Scotch eggs

Minced venison is increasingly available in supermarkets as people seek out lean alternatives to beef and lamb. It is so lean, in fact, that it needs the meat from a good-quality sausage to help bind it together and stop it being too dry when wrapped around the eggs. These special Scotch eggs may seem like a bit of a faff, but they are absolutely worth the effort for a tasty starter or picnic.

1. Heat the oil in a small saucepan over a low heat, add the shallots and cook for 5–8 minutes, until completely soft (see Tip). Pour off the excess oil, then drain the shallots on kitchen paper and leave to cool.

2. Bring a saucepan of water to the boil and add six of the eggs. Bring back to the boil and cook for 5 minutes. Using a slotted spoon, transfer the eggs to a bowl of iced water. Once they are cool enough to handle, drain, then carefully peel off the shells. Set aside.

3. Meanwhile, place the cooled shallots, the minced venison, sausage meat, ground spices, garlic, chopped herbs, cream, salt and pepper in a large bowl, and mix everything together thoroughly with your hands. Divide the minced meat mixture into six even portions and shape into flattened ovals. Press each portion evenly around a peeled egg, enclosing the egg completely.

4. Preheat the oven to 200°C/180°C fan/Gas 6 and heat a deep-fat fryer to 180°C or fill a large saucepan one-third full of vegetable oil and heat until a cube of bread dropped in the oil sizzles and turns golden in 30 seconds.

5. Meanwhile, beat the remaining egg in a shallow dish and place the breadcrumbs in another shallow dish. Roll the mince-covered eggs in the beaten egg, allowing any excess to drip off, then coat in the breadcrumbs, pressing them in so that they really stick.

6. Deep-fry the coated eggs (in batches) in the hot oil for 4 minutes, until golden all over. Remove with a slotted spoon, then drain on kitchen paper. Once they are all deep-fried, place the Scotch eggs on a baking tray and bake in the oven for about 8 minutes, until cooked through inside and golden brown and crisp on the outside. Serve warm or cold with chutney.

MAKES 6 SCOTCH EGGS

1 tbsp vegetable oil, plus extra for deep-frying

2 banana shallots, finely chopped

7 eggs

1kg minced venison

1 sausage, skin removed

2 tsp ground coriander

2 tsp ground cumin

2 tsp ground nutmeg

1 garlic clove, crushed

4 parsley sprigs, leaves picked and chopped

2 tarragon sprigs, leaves picked and chopped

100ml double cream

2 tsp sea salt

1 tsp freshly ground black pepper

100g panko or ordinary breadcrumbs

TIP
An alternative way to cook the shallots is to put them into a microwaveable bowl with the vegetable oil and cover with cling film (leaving a small air gap). Place in the microwave and cook on high for 2 minutes. Drain and cool as above.

# THE BIG WEEKEND

Bread Street changes at the weekend as we welcome a different crowd to our weekday regulars. Families and groups of friends, local residents and out-of-towners come for our roast lunches, chargrilled steaks and burgers then hang around for pudding and cheese and coffee and just one more drink… The atmosphere is laid-back and sociable and the focus is on having a good time. Sometimes there is live music and every Sunday we have face painters and a house magician to entertain the kids. Everyone seems to be just a little bit less serious than they are in the week.

It's great going out for lunch at the weekend but even better staying at home and preparing your own crowd-pleasing feasts. We suspect that this is when most of the real cooking happens at home, when busy people finally find some time to roll up their sleeves and slip an apron over their heads. Cookbooks are studied, new recipes are tried, barbecues are lit and friends pile in to enjoy the dividends.

Feeding lots of people can be daunting but half the battle is choosing the right dishes to cook. Pick robust cuts of meat that can endure long slow cooking at low temperatures or sauces that can be made in advance and drizzled over barbecued chicken or steak at the last minute. Roast beef is the ultimate weekend meal and we consider ourselves experts – try our foolproof roast sirloin and serve it with spiced carrots and Yorkshire puddings. Follow with big puds for sharing like trifle, Eton mess and sticky toffee pudding and wash everything down with big jugs of refreshing cocktails – the recipe for a perfect weekend. The washing-up can wait…

# THE BIG WEEKEND

# The BSK burger

It's the combination of different cuts of beef and the minced fat running through the mixture that makes our burgers famously good. Ask your butcher to mince the beef for you or invest in a mincer for a lifetime of great burgers. If you can't get hold of the different cuts, regular minced beef will still work a treat. The Char Siu butter is optional, but it's seriously tasty and makes the burgers even more juicy.

1. Put the minced cuts of beef into a large bowl and mix together using your hands, adding the fat a little at a time, making sure you don't overmix. Divide the mixture into four equal portions and roll each portion into a ball. Press the balls down gently with your hands to form patties. Leave the burgers at room temperature for about 10 minutes before cooking.

2. Season the burgers on both sides with plenty of salt and pepper. Heat a dash of vegetable oil in a large frying pan until hot, add the burgers and pan-fry for 5 minutes on each side for medium or 8–10 minutes for well done. Alternatively, brush the burgers with a little oil and cook them over a preheated barbecue.

3. Meanwhile, preheat the grill to high.

4. For an unctuous, tasty addition, make the Char Siu butter, if you like. Simply mix together all the ingredients in a bowl until combined, then put a tablespoon of the butter on top of each cooked burger.

5. Put two slices of cheese (per burger) on top of the butter (if you are not using the Char Siu butter, just put the cheese directly on the cooked burgers), then place under the hot grill to melt.

6. Slice the burger buns in half and toast them lightly before layering the butter- or cheese-topped burgers, lettuce leaves, slices of tomato and some gherkin, then place the bun lids on top. Serve immediately.

SERVES 4

200g minced short rib

400g minced chuck

200g minced brisket

80g minced beef fat

Vegetable oil, for frying

8 slices of Monterey Jack cheese (or use Cheddar or Gouda)

4 burger buns, such as brioche buns

1 little gem lettuce, separated into leaves

3 plum tomatoes, sliced

2 gherkins, thinly sliced lengthways

Sea salt and freshly ground black pepper

*For the Char Siu butter (optional)*

75g butter, softened

1 tsp runny honey

2 tsp hoisin sauce

2 tsp black bean paste or sauce

1–2 garlic cloves, crushed

# Spatchcocked poussins

*with chimichurri sauce*

A poussin is a young chicken which is just the right size for one person. Spatchcocking (or splitting open, then flattening) poussins or other poultry or game birds will ensure that they cook more quickly and evenly on a barbecue or griddle pan. Doing this yourself is straightforward and a great way to improve your knife skills, but if you don't have time, ask your butcher to do it for you. You could also do this recipe with a larger chicken, but remember to increase the cooking time.

1. Preheat the oven to 200°C/180°C fan/Gas 6.

2. Thread each poussin with 2 skewers to keep it flat. Do this by threading each skewer through a bit of a breast and a thigh, then repeat with the other skewer so the skewers cross. Rub all over the poussins with olive oil and season with salt and pepper. Set aside.

3. To make the chimichurri sauce, put the shallots, parsley, jalapeño peppers, oregano and chives into a blender, and blitz together, or finely chop them by hand and mix together well. Add the olive oil, sherry vinegar, Tabasco and salt to taste, and pulse to combine, or mix well by hand. Adjust the seasonings to taste.

4. Preheat a barbecue or place a large griddle pan over a high heat. When the barbecue is hot or the griddle pan is smoking, place the flattened poussins on the grill or in the pan (you may need to do this in batches), skin side down, and cook for 3–4 minutes, until golden. Turn the poussins over and cook for a further 3–4 minutes.

5. Transfer the poussins to two roasting trays with 50ml of the chicken stock in each tray. Roast in the oven for 15–20 minutes or until the poussin juices run clear. Leave the poussins to rest for at least 5 minutes before serving.

6. Meanwhile, grill the lemon halves, cut side down, on the barbecue or griddle pan for a few minutes, until lightly charred.

7. Serve the whole poussins covered with a generous amount of the chimichurri sauce and the lemon halves alongside.

SERVES 6

6 poussins, spatchcocked (see Tip)

Olive oil

100ml chicken stock

3 lemons, halved

Sea salt and freshly ground black pepper

*For the chimichurri sauce*

150g shallots, finely chopped

50g fresh parsley leaves

70g fresh green jalapeño peppers, roughly chopped (leave the seeds in, if you like it hot; remove them if not)

10g fresh oregano leaves

30g chives, roughly snipped

6–8 tbsp extra virgin olive oil

About 1 tbsp sherry vinegar, or to taste

2 dashes of Tabasco sauce, or to taste

TIP
To spatchcock a poussin, put the bird on a chopping board, breast side down, with the legs towards you. Using a strong pair of kitchen scissors or poultry shears, cut each side of the parson's nose and down the length of the bird either side of the backbone. Cut through the rib bones so you can remove the backbone in one piece. Open out the poussin, turn it over and flatten by pressing down firmly with the heel of your hand.

# Whole baked brill

Presenting guests with a whole baked fish is always impressive, especially when covered with golden potato scales. If you can't get brill, this method works equally well with turbot or halibut, but be aware that the cooking time will vary depending on the size and thickness of the fish.

1. Preheat the oven to 200°C/180°C fan/Gas 6.

2. Wash two of the potatoes, then using a mandolin or very sharp knife, slice each very thinly. Place the slices in a bowl with a pinch of salt and 1 tablespoon of oil, then leave to soften for 10 minutes.

3. Take the remaining two potatoes and peel them. Dice each one into 1cm cubes, then put into a bowl with the remaining olive oil, season well with salt and pepper and toss to coat.

4. Stuff the fish cavity with one thyme sprig and a third of the garlic slices, then season inside and outside the fish with salt and pepper.

5. Set aside half of the nice-looking, smaller potato slices, as these will be used to mimic the scales of the fish. Place the remaining slices over the bottom of a non-stick roasting tray, overlapping slightly (if the tray isn't non-stick, line it with baking parchment). Place the fish on top, then arrange the remaining sliced potatoes onto the fish, overlapping them slightly to resemble the scales.

6. Arrange the diced potatoes around the fish, then sprinkle over the remaining thyme and garlic. Add 50ml water and the wine to the roasting tray. Cook in the oven for 30–40 minutes, until the fish is cooked through and the potatoes are nice and golden.

7. Remove from the oven, remove the potatoes from the top of the fish and reserve, then carefully fillet the fish. Using a sharp fish or filleting knife, slice down the middle of the fish from the head to the tail, using the tip of the knife to feel where the backbone is, sliding the knife down along one side of it. Lift the fillet with a fish slice – it should come away cleanly. Do the same on the other side of the backbone to remove the second fillet. Then, to remove the other two fillets, carefully turn the fish over and do the same again.

8. Serve the fish fillets with the crunchy sliced and diced potatoes alongside. Spoon some of the sauce left in the roasting tray over the fish. This is delicious served with a fennel and mixed leaf salad (add some capers too, if you like) dressed with a citronette dressing (see Tip).

SERVES 4

4 roasting potatoes (about 700g), such as King Edward or Desirée, unpeeled

50ml extra virgin olive oil

1 whole brill, about 800g–1kg, cleaned and scaled (ask your fishmonger to do this for you)

4 thyme sprigs

3 garlic cloves, sliced

50ml white wine

Sea salt and freshly ground black pepper

TIP
To make a citronette dressing, lightly whisk together one part lemon juice and three parts extra virgin olive oil until combined, then season with a little salt.

# Roast beef

*with caramelised onion gravy*

A weekend wouldn't feel like a proper weekend without a really good roast lunch, and roast beef is our absolute favourite. When cooking, the quality of the ingredients is very important and this is never more so than when roasting meat… buy the best beef you can afford and you are halfway there. Resting is equally essential, so don't be tempted to cut this short. Be patient and you will be rewarded with juicier, more tender results. If you like, roast the beef on a bed of mixed root vegetables.

1. Rub the garlic halves and thyme leaves all over the beef. Place the joint in a large dish, drizzle over the olive oil, then rub it into the meat all over. Cover and leave to marinate in the fridge for 1–2 days before you cook it (you don't have to marinate the beef in advance, but it does make it super tasty! – see Tip). Take the beef out of the fridge about an hour before cooking, to let it come up to room temperature.

2. Preheat the oven to 190°C/170°C fan/Gas 5.

3. Preheat a dry frying pan until very hot, then sear the beef over a high heat until it's coloured on all sides. Place the beef in a large, hob-proof roasting tray with the garlic halves and the thyme sprig and roast for about 45 minutes for medium rare (or until it reaches 45–47°C in the centre, if you have a meat thermometer). Add 10–12 minutes for medium (or until it reaches 55–60°C in the centre), or add about 20 minutes if you like it well done (or until it reaches 65–70°C in the centre).

4. Transfer the beef to a warm platter, cover loosely with foil and leave to rest for at least 20 minutes, and anything up to 40 minutes, before serving.

5. Meanwhile, to make the gravy, place the roasting tray over a low heat on the hob, add the onions to the juices in the tray and cook gently for about 20 minutes, stirring occasionally, until really soft and caramelised. Stir in the flour until combined, then whisk in the red wine, making sure there are no lumps. Bring to the boil, whisking, then bubble rapidly until the red wine has reduced by half. Stir in the hot stock, then cook over a medium heat for about 8 minutes, stirring occasionally, until reduced to a thick gravy.

6. Carve the beef thinly and pour the gravy into a warm jug. Serve with Yorkshire Puddings (see page 121) and steamed chard.

SERVES 6-8

1 head of garlic (about 12 cloves), cut in half

5 thyme sprigs, leaves picked, plus 1 extra

1.8kg beef sirloin

3–4 tbsp olive oil

4 large onions, sliced

150g plain flour

500ml red wine

1.5 litres hot beef stock

TIP
If you prefer not to marinate the beef before cooking, simply place the garlic/thyme and oil-rubbed joint of beef in a large roasting tray. Continue to sear and roast as in step 3 onwards.

# Yorkshire puddings

The secret to a successful Yorkshire pudding is allowing the batter to rest before pouring it into very hot oil. In the restaurant, we make our batter the night before and leave it at room temperature until it's needed the following day. You don't need to do this, but make sure you rest yours for at least an hour before you cook to ensure a good rise and deliciously light puddings.

1. Beat the eggs together in a mixing bowl using a balloon whisk. Sift the flour with the salt, then gradually beat this into the eggs to make a smooth batter. Whisk in the milk until combined. Cover and leave to stand at room temperature for about 1 hour.

2. Preheat the oven to 220°C/200°C fan/Gas 7. Put 2 teaspoons of vegetable oil into each compartment of two 4-hole Yorkshire pudding tins (see Tip). If you only have one tin, you'll have to do this in two batches. Place the tin in the oven for 12–15 minutes to heat up the oil and tins until very hot. This is important for the rise.

3. Stir the batter and pour into a jug. At the oven (this is safer than carrying a tin of hot oil across the kitchen), carefully pour some batter into the middle of the oil in each hole, remembering that it is very hot. Watch out as the oil will sizzle a bit as the batter hits it. Put the tins straight back into the oven and bake for about 15 minutes or until the Yorkshires are well risen, golden brown and crisp.

4. Serve immediately with Roast Beef with Caramelised Onion Gravy (see page 118) and all the trimmings.

MAKES 8 LARGE
YORKSHIRES

3 large eggs
125g plain flour
½ tsp sea salt
150ml whole milk
Vegetable oil

TIP
To make 14–16 smaller Yorkshire puddings, put 1 teaspoon of vegetable oil into each hole of a deep muffin tin (each cup measuring about 7cm diameter x 2.5cm deep), then heat up as described in step 2, before pouring in the batter. Bake the Yorkshires for 12–15 minutes.

# Slow-roasted pork belly
## *with spiced apple sauce*

This method for roasting pork belly – hot to begin with, cooler for a longer period of time, then a hot blast at the end – guarantees the most excellent crispy crackling, as well as meltingly tender meat. It is important to score the skin before you cook the pork to achieve really crispy crackling, and a very sharp knife is fundamental for this. The cinnamon-spiced apple sauce provides the perfect accompaniment, too.

1. Preheat the oven to 240°C/220°C fan/Gas 9.

2. Using a very sharp knife, score the skin of the pork belly widthways in lines that are about 1cm apart from each other, making sure that you don't cut all the way through to the meat (otherwise it will burn).

3. Place the scored pork belly onto a wire rack placed inside a roasting tray. Squeeze the lemon juice over the skin. Sprinkle a generous amount of salt evenly over the skin and then pour the vegetable oil on top of the salt. Massage the salt, lemon juice and oil into the skin, making sure there are no puddles of oil left on top.

4. Roast the pork belly in the oven for 25–30 minutes, until the skin has started to crisp up. Reduce the oven temperature to 160°C/140°C fan/Gas 3 and roast for a further 1½ hours, until the meat is cooked and tender. Increase the oven temperature back to 240°C/220°C fan/Gas 9 and roast for a further 15 minutes or so, to make sure the crackling is very crisp and deep golden in colour.

5. While the pork belly is roasting, make the apple and cinnamon sauce. Put the apples in a pan with 2–3 tablespoons of water. Cover and cook over a low heat for 10–15 minutes, until the apples are soft and beginning to catch on the bottom of the pan (to add a bit of colour). Add a little more water if the apples are catching too much.

6. Once the apples are cooked, remove from the heat and stir through the cinnamon then blitz with a stick blender for a smooth sauce or leave whole for a chunkier accompaniment. Leave to cool.

7. Carve the pork and serve with the apple sauce, making sure everyone gets some crispy crackling too.

SERVES 6-8

1 pork belly on the bone, about 2–3kg

Juice of ¼ lemon

Sea salt

25ml vegetable oil

*For the apple and cinnamon sauce*

500g dessert apples, such as Braeburn, peeled, cored and roughly chopped

½ tsp ground cinnamon, or to taste

# The perfect steak

All chefs have cooked a lot of steaks, we could do it in our sleep, but there are many tips we can pass onto cooks of every level that will ensure restaurant-quality results every time. Make sure the pan is hot enough to give a really deep caramelised colour to the meat – the deeper the colour the more flavourful the cooked steak – and don't overcrowd the pan if you are cooking more than one steak. Remember too that resting properly is just as important as cooking – cutting into the steak too early will release all those tasty juices.

1. Remove the steak from the fridge 15–20 minutes before cooking, to allow the meat to come to room temperature.

2. Meanwhile, make the Béarnaise sauce. Put the red and white wine vinegars into a pan with the shallot and herb stalks (reserve the chopped tarragon leaves for later). Bring to the boil, then bubble over a medium heat until reduced to about 1 tablespoon liquid, about 5 minutes. Set aside to cool, then strain.

3. Meanwhile, clarify the butter. Melt the butter in a small pan over a low heat. Remove from the heat and cool slightly, then carefully pour off the yellow liquid butter, discarding the white solids left at the bottom. Leave to cool.

4. Put the egg yolks and reduced vinegar into a heatproof bowl set over a pan of barely simmering water over a very low heat (making sure the base of the bowl doesn't touch the water). Whisk until pale and beginning to thicken, about 2 minutes. Slowly whisk in the clarified butter, a little at a time, until the mixture thickens and emulsifies. Remove from the heat. Season to taste with salt and pepper and stir in the chopped tarragon before serving.

5. Brush or rub the steak all over with a little oil, then season on both sides with salt and pepper. Preheat a heavy-based non-stick frying pan over a medium–high heat.

6. Place the steak in the hot pan and sear for 3–4 minutes without moving it. Turn the steak over and cook it on the other side for 2–3 minutes, again without moving it. Add the butter along with the thyme and garlic, and baste the steak with the melted butter for 30–60 seconds.

7. Transfer the steak to a plate or chopping board and leave to rest for 3–4 minutes with the thyme and garlic on top of it. Slice the steak at an angle, season with salt and pepper, then serve with the Béarnaise sauce.

SERVES 2

1 sirloin or rib eye steak, about 350g and 2–2.5cm thick (trimmed of excess fat, if you like)
Drizzle of olive oil (about 1 tsp)
15g butter
2–3 thyme sprigs
2 garlic cloves, bashed
Sea salt and freshly ground black pepper

*For the Béarnaise sauce*
3 tbsp red wine vinegar
3 tbsp white wine vinegar
1 shallot, very finely chopped
Small handful of fresh parsley stalks
Small handful of fresh tarragon sprigs, leaves picked and chopped and stalks retained (you should have about 1–2 tbsp chopped tarragon)
175g butter
3 large egg yolks
Sea salt and freshly ground black pepper

TIPS
These cooking instructions are for a steak served medium rare. If you prefer your steak more cooked, leave it longer in the pan or finish it in a hot oven.

Be careful not to overheat the egg yolk mixture when making the sauce or it may split and curdle. If it does, whisk in an ice cube and it should re-combine. If it has completely curdled, put a fresh egg yolk into a clean heatproof bowl and place over the pan of water. Whisk, then add to the curdled mixture, 1 tablespoon at a time, until the mixture emulsifies.

# Spiced carrots

Forget boring old boiled carrots with your Sunday lunch; instead toss them in brown sugar and ground spices and roast them in a hot oven to bring out their natural sweetness. The spices add a lovely Middle Eastern flavour but can be left out if you prefer.

1. Preheat the oven to 220°C/200°C fan/Gas 7.

2. Mix the ground spices and sugar together in a small bowl. Stir in the oil.

3. Lay the carrots on a large baking tray or in a large, shallow roasting tray. Pour over the spice mix, season with some salt, then toss everything together to mix. Spread the carrots out in an even layer.

4. Roast for 25–30 minutes, until just tender and golden, giving them a quick stir about halfway through. Garnish with a sprinkle of chopped parsley and serve.

SERVES 6-8 AS A SIDE DISH

1 tsp ground cumin

1 tsp ground cinnamon

1 tsp ground star anise (see Tip)

2 tsp light soft brown sugar

5 tbsp vegetable oil

1kg carrots, peeled and cut into long diagonal slices, each about 1.5cm thick

Sea salt

Chopped fresh flat leaf parsley, to garnish

TIP
If you don't have ground star anise, grind a few whole star anise to a powder using a pestle and mortar.

# Garlicky mashed potatoes

Take delicious, creamy mashed potatoes and make them extra tasty by folding through some crushed garlic. When it's in season, we make this with wild garlic leaves, which is also fantastic. Wild garlic grows abundantly in the British countryside during the spring, so go foraging for your own – you will need a couple of handfuls or so. Remember to wash the leaves thoroughly, then pat them dry before puréeing with a little olive oil.

1. Put the peeled potatoes into a large pan with enough cold water to cover them, then bring to the boil. Reduce the heat and simmer for 15–20 minutes, until the potatoes are tender when pierced with a knife.

2. Meanwhile, heat the milk and cream together in a small pan, just until small bubbles appear around the edge of the pan. Remove from the heat, stir in the garlic, and leave to infuse for about 5 minutes.

3. In the meantime, drain the potatoes and push through a ricer or a mouli, or use a potato masher. Return the mashed potatoes to the pan, then beat in the butter until combined.

4. Pour the infused milk/cream mixture over the mashed potatoes, mixing it in well. Season to taste with salt and, if necessary, warm through briefly over a gentle heat before serving.

SERVES 4 (*easily doubled*)

1kg King Edward, Desirée or red-skinned potatoes, peeled and chopped into large chunks

100ml whole milk

100ml double cream

1 plump garlic clove, crushed

100g butter

Sea salt

TIP

To make wild garlic mash, put two handfuls of wild garlic leaves and 1 tablespoon of olive oil into a blender and blitz together to make a purée (use this purée in place of the garlic). Heat the milk and cream until almost boiling, then mix into the mashed potatoes. Beat in the butter, then fold through the wild garlic purée and season with salt.

# Triple-cooked chips

We're famous for our chips at Bread Street, and having tried many different methods, we can confirm that it is definitely worth cooking them three times for the best results. The finished chip is soft in the middle, super crunchy on the outside and a delicious golden colour all over. We like them cut really chunky, and served with home-made mayonnaise (see page 132) and an ice-cold beer.

SERVES 6-8 AS A SIDE DISH

2kg chipping potatoes, such as Agria or Maris Piper

Sea salt

Vegetable oil, for deep-frying

1. Peel the potatoes and cut them into large wedges or batons. Wash the starch off the chips under cold running water until the water runs clear.

2. Bring a large pan of salted water to the boil. Add the potato wedges or batons, bring back to the boil and cook for 10–12 minutes or until they are soft when you insert a sharp knife but still remain intact. Drain and leave the potatoes to cool on kitchen paper.

3. Heat a deep-fat fryer to 140°C or fill a large saucepan one-third full of vegetable oil and heat to 140°C (the oil doesn't need to be really hot at this stage, as this step is to cook the chips through rather than crisp and colour them). Deep-fry the chips in small batches for 8 minutes, then remove and leave them to drain and cool on kitchen paper again.

4. When you are ready to serve, reheat the deep-fat fryer to 180°C or reheat the oil in the saucepan until a cube of bread dropped in the oil sizzles and turns golden in 30 seconds.

5. Deep-fry the chips in small batches again for 8–10 minutes, until golden and crispy. Drain well and season with salt, then serve.

# Mayonnaise

This is the Bread Street Kitchen base recipe for mayonnaise with three suggestions for flavouring it, from the more subtle tarragon to the fiery sriracha (tangy Thai chilli sauce), to the aromatic harissa (North African hot and spicy red chilli paste). All three are excellent served with our Triple-cooked chips (see page 130). The trick to making a lovely firm mayonnaise is to add the oil in a slow, steady stream, whisking all the time – too much oil added at once will cause the mayonnaise to split.

1. Put the egg yolk, mustard, vinegar and lemon juice into a bowl, and beat together until combined (or blend together in a food processor).

2. Gradually pour in the oil in a slow, steady stream, whisking all the time (or pour in the oil through the feeder tube, blending continuously, if using a food processor) until the mixture thickens. If the mayonnaise becomes too thick, add a little hot water and then continue adding the oil.

3. Once all the oil has been added, thin to the required consistency with a little hot water, if necessary, then season to taste with salt and pepper, checking to see if it needs a little more lemon juice.

4. The mayonnaise can now be served as it is or one of a choice of flavourings can be added.

5. To make tarragon mayonnaise, stir the tarragon leaves into the mayonnaise until combined. To make harissa mayonnaise, stir the harissa paste into the mayonnaise until well combined. To make Sriracha mayonnaise, stir the sriracha sauce and tomato ketchup into the mayonnaise, mixing well until combined.

SERVES 10

1 egg yolk

1 tsp Dijon mustard

1 tsp white wine vinegar

Juice of ½ lemon

200ml vegetable oil or mild olive oil

Sea salt and freshly ground black pepper

*For tarragon mayonnaise*

3 tarragon sprigs, leaves picked and finely chopped

*For harissa mayonnaise*

50g harissa paste

*For Sriracha mayonnaise*

100g Sriracha sauce

150g tomato ketchup

TIP
The mayonnaise will keep in a screw-top jar in the fridge for up to 3 days.

# Braised asparagus, peas and green beans

The reason why vegetable side dishes like this one taste so good in restaurants is that they are cooked in such a generous amount of butter. You can reduce the butter content if you want to be a bit healthier, but the finished dish won't be quite as delicious! Halve all the ingredient quantities if you are serving fewer people.

1. Melt the butter in a large saucepan or sauté pan. Add the shallots and cook gently for 4–5 minutes, stirring occasionally, until softened.

2. Add the green beans to the pan and cook over a medium heat for 2 minutes. Tip in the asparagus and peas. Pour over the hot stock, then cover and simmer for a further 3 minutes, until the vegetables are just tender. Season to taste with salt and pepper, then serve with the buttery juices spooned over.

SERVES 6-8 AS A SIDE DISH

100g butter

2 shallots, finely sliced

200g green beans, trimmed and each cut in half

2 bunches of asparagus, each spear cut diagonally into three

200g fresh podded peas (you will need about 500g peas in their pods – see Tip)

400ml hot vegetable stock

Sea salt and freshly ground black pepper

TIP
Use frozen peas if you can't find fresh ones.

# Kohlrabi coleslaw

Or should that be Kohlslaw? This crunchy healthy side salad is a refreshing accompaniment to the BSK burger on page 113, The perfect steak on page 125, or the Spatchcocked poussins on page 114. Labneh is a soft, cream cheese-like strained yoghurt, similar to but thicker than standard natural Greek yoghurt, though the dressing can be made with this too if you can't get hold of labneh.

1. Put the yoghurt, mustard and cream into a large serving bowl and mix together.

2. Add the kohlrabi, celery, carrot, onion and herbs, and mix everything together until the vegetables are thoroughly coated in the dressing. Stir through 2–3 tablespoons of cold water to thin down the dressing a little, if necessary.

3. Add the lemon zest and mix, then season with salt. Serve.

SERVES 6-8 AS A SIDE DISH

150g labneh or natural
    Greek yoghurt

1 tbsp wholegrain mustard

50ml double cream

1 kohlrabi (about 250g),
    trimmed, peeled and cut
    into julienne

1 celery stick, trimmed
    and cut into julienne

1 carrot, peeled and
    cut into julienne

1 small red onion, finely sliced

Handful of flat leaf parsley, torn

Handful of coriander leaves, torn

Finely grated zest of 1 lemon

Sea salt

# Strawberry trifles

Trifle is a proper pudding for a celebration and is perfect for serving a crowd. But trifles aren't just for Christmas – this version is made with strawberries, elderflower and basil for a lovely taste of summer. It takes a bit of time and effort to put all the elements together, but it really is well worth it. You can leave out the gin if you are catering for children.

8 boudoir biscuits or
   sponge fingers

1 tbsp gin

*For the jelly*

450g fresh strawberries,
   quartered

125g caster sugar

180ml elderflower cordial,
   mixed with 70ml water
   to make 250ml

6 sheets of leaf gelatine

*For the custard*

300ml double cream

Seeds from ½ vanilla pod

3 large egg yolks

30g caster sugar

*For the macerated strawberries*

25g caster sugar

250g strawberries,
   halved if large

1 tbsp good-quality
   balsamic glaze

2 fresh basil leaves, chopped

*To decorate*

Freeze-dried strawberries
   (optional)

Fresh basil sprigs or leaves,
   shredded (optional)

1. To make the jelly, put the strawberries into a pan with the sugar and 1 tablespoon of water. Cover and cook gently until soft, about 8 minutes. Pour into a blender and blitz until smooth (or use a stick blender in the pan). Rest a sieve over a bowl, spoon in the strawberry mixture, then stir with a wooden spoon to extract the puréed juice.

2. Weigh out 250ml of this juice and mix with the diluted elderflower cordial, reserving the remaining strawberry juice to use for soaking the boudoir biscuits. Place the gelatine leaves in a small bowl of cold water and leave for about 3–5 minutes, until softened.

3. Meanwhile, pour the strawberry and cordial mix into a saucepan, and bring to the boil. Remove from the heat. Squeeze out the gelatine and add to the saucepan, whisking well until it is completely dissolved. Pour the jelly into a large glass bowl or divide among individual glasses, then leave to set in the fridge for at least 3 hours.

4. To make the custard, pour the cream into a saucepan, add the vanilla and bring to the boil over a medium heat. Put the egg yolks and sugar into a heatproof bowl, and stir using a spatula.

5. Pour half of the cream onto the egg-yolk mix, stirring constantly, then return the mixture to the remaining cream in the pan, stirring as you go. Cook gently, stirring continuously, until the custard is thickened enough to coat the back of a wooden spoon (65–70°C); do not let it boil. Pour into a bowl, then cool quickly in the fridge.

6. Meanwhile, put the caster sugar into a large bowl and add 25ml of water. Stir to help dissolve the sugar. Stir in the strawberries, balsamic glaze and basil, then leave to macerate for about 30 minutes.

7. To assemble the trifle, sit the boudoir biscuits on top of the jelly in a single layer, breaking to fit if using individual glasses. Mix the reserved strawberry juice with the gin and pour evenly over the biscuits. Transfer the bowl or glasses to the fridge to chill briefly.

8. Pour the cold custard over the soaked biscuits to cover them evenly. Return to the fridge until you're ready to decorate the top.

9. To serve, strain the macerated strawberries and spoon over the custard. Decorate with freeze-dried strawberries and basil, if you like.

# Monkey Shoulder cheesecake

Monkey Shoulder is a blended malt whisky that is smooth, sweet and very easy to drink… or to put into cheesecake! It tastes very mild when combined with the cream cheese filling and it goes brilliantly with the ginger biscuit base. Monkey Shoulder is widely available, but you can easily replace it with a whisky of your choice. If you are planning to share this with children, leave the whisky out – it will still be delicious.

1. Grease the base of a 23cm springform tin or deep loose-based round tin and set aside. For the biscuit base, melt the butter in a pan over a low heat. Remove from the heat, stir in the crushed biscuits and sugar until combined, then press the mixture evenly over the bottom of the prepared tin. Chill in the fridge for at least 30 minutes.

2. Put all the ingredients for the cheesecake topping, except the whisky, in a mixing bowl and whisk together using an electric mixer, until smooth and quite thick. Pour in the whisky and whisk again until the mixture is the consistency of thickly whipped cream.

3. Pour the topping over the biscuit base and smooth the top, then transfer to the fridge and leave to set for a minimum of 3 hours or overnight.

4. Warm the cherries or berries and sugar in a saucepan with 1 tablespoon water until they begin to soften. Cool.

5. Once set, carefully remove the cheesecake from the tin and transfer to a serving plate, drizzle over the fruit and syrup, then slice to serve.

SERVES 8-10

*For the biscuit base*

75g butter, plus extra for greasing

200g ginger nut biscuits, smashed to fine crumbs

25g caster sugar

*For the cheesecake topping*

300g cream cheese or full-fat soft cheese, softened for an hour out of the fridge

130g caster sugar

Seeds from 2 vanilla pods

250ml double cream

150g crème fraîche

2 tbsp Monkey Shoulder whisky or other whisky of your choice

*To serve*

300g cherries, halved and stoned, or seasonal berries

2 tbsp caster sugar

# Strawberry, nectarine and rosewater Eton mess

Eton mess has become a British summertime institution like Wimbledon, the Boat Race and the Chelsea Flower Show, so it would be unthinkable not to put it on the menu as soon as British strawberries come into season. To further celebrate the summer, we add nectarines as well as a few drops of rosewater to our meringue mixture, which gives the whole dessert a lovely aroma of fresh rose petals with a hint of Turkish delight.

1. First make the coulis. Put the cherries, strawberries or berries into a pan with the sugar and cook over a low–medium heat, stirring occasionally, until the sugar has dissolved, 3–4 minutes. Increase the heat to medium and let the mixture bubble gently until the fruit is soft and broken down, about 3 minutes. Remove from the heat. Blitz the fruit in a blender (or use a stick blender in the pan), then push through a fine sieve placed over a bowl to create a smooth coulis. Stir in the lemon juice. Set aside to cool, then chill before serving (see Tip).

2. Meanwhile, preheat the oven to 140°C/120°C fan/Gas 1. Line a baking sheet with baking parchment.

3. For the meringue, whisk the egg whites in a large, grease-free bowl until they form soft peaks. Mix both sugars together, then gradually add them to the egg whites, a tablespoon at a time, whisking continuously, until the mixture forms stiff peaks. Whisk in the rosewater. The mixture should be thick, smooth and glossy.

4. Scrape the meringue onto the centre of the prepared baking sheet and spread out evenly to form a circle about 20cm in diameter. Bake for 1 hour 20 minutes, until crisp on the outside and a little soft in the middle. Transfer to a wire rack (still on the paper) and leave to cool completely.

5. Make the Chantilly cream. Put the cream, icing sugar and vanilla seeds into a mixing bowl and whisk together until the mixture forms soft peaks.

6. To assemble the Eton mess, spoon the Chantilly cream onto a large serving board or plate. Break the meringue into shards and stick the pieces into the cream. Decorate with sliced strawberries and nectarines and drizzle the strawberry coulis over the top. Scatter with mint leaves and serve.

SERVES 6

*For the coulis*

250g cherries, pitted, strawberries or berries, cut into quarters, or frozen berries

75g caster sugar

1 tbsp lemon juice

*For the meringue*

2 large egg whites

70g icing sugar, sifted

70g caster sugar

5 drops of rosewater

*For the Chantilly cream*

500ml double cream

4 tbsp icing sugar

Seeds from 1 vanilla pod

*To decorate*

150g strawberries, cut into quarters

2 nectarines or peaches, sliced

Fresh mint leaves or small sprigs, or a few fresh rose petals

TIPS

The coulis can be made up to a day ahead and kept in an airtight container in the fridge. Leftover coulis can be stored in the fridge for up to 3 days, and drizzled over ice cream or mixed seasonal fresh berries.

For a daintier presentation, you could assemble single portions on individual plates.

# Sticky toffee pudding

*with banana caramel sauce*

Being in the City of London, our old-fashioned nursery puddings are always popular, the stickier and more comforting, the better. Our sticky toffee pudding is exactly how it should be – soft and squidgy with plenty of banana caramel sauce to pool on top. Serve with clotted cream or crème fraîche and a big smile.

1. Preheat the oven to 190°C/170°C fan/Gas 5. Grease and line the base of a 30 x 23 x 4cm deep baking tin with baking parchment.

2. Put the dates into a saucepan with 225ml water. Cook over a low–medium heat until soft and mushy, and the water is almost all absorbed, 4–5 minutes. Transfer to a blender or use a stick blender in the pan and blitz to a purée, then leave to cool slightly.

3. Whisk the brown sugar and eggs together in a large bowl for a minute or so, until a bit paler in colour and light, then whisk in the melted butter to combine. Sift the flour, baking powder and bicarbonate of soda together in a separate bowl, then stir this into the egg mixture, a third at a time, using a large metal spoon. Stir in the date purée until combined. The mixture will be soft. Pour it into the prepared tin, spreading gently to smooth the surface. Bake for 25–30 minutes, until risen and firm but springy to the touch.

4. While the pudding is baking, make the banana caramel sauce. Combine all the ingredients, except the bananas, in a large saucepan and heat gently until the sugar has dissolved and the butter has melted, stirring often. Increase the heat to medium and bring to a fast simmer, then bubble for 1–2 minutes, just to thicken the sauce slightly. Remove from the heat and leave to cool for a bit.

5. Pour the sauce into a blender (or use a stick blender in the pan), add the chopped bananas, if using, and blitz together until smooth and combined. Warm through gently before serving.

6. Check the pudding is cooked by inserting a knife into the centre – it should come out clean. Remove the pudding from the oven and turn out onto a wire rack. Peel off the lining paper, invert the pudding onto a board, then cut into 12 squares to serve. Alternatively, cool the pudding slightly in the tin, then cut into squares and remove the portions, leaving the lining paper behind.

7. Pour some of the sauce over each portion (don't be shy), then drizzle extra on the plates. Serve with a dollop of clotted cream or crème fraîche.

SERVES 12

*For the pudding*
325g stoned dates, roughly chopped
275g dark soft brown sugar or dark muscovado sugar
3 large eggs
90g butter, melted and cooled slightly, plus extra for greasing
300g self-raising flour
1 tsp baking powder
1 tsp bicarbonate of soda

*For the banana caramel sauce*
300g butter, cut into pieces
375g light soft brown sugar
150g dark soft brown sugar or dark muscovado sugar
375ml double cream
2 just ripe bananas, chopped (optional)

Clotted cream or crème fraîche, to serve

TIPS
The pudding can be made a day or two ahead. Simply make it as directed, then cool completely before wrapping it well and storing in a cool, dry place. The sauce can also be made ahead and kept in the fridge, then reheated gently to serve.

Any pudding or sauce leftovers will freeze well (separately) for up to 1 month. Thaw at a cool room temperature, then gently reheat to serve.

# Banana upside-down cake

This is definitely more of a pudding than a cake and should be served fresh from the oven, while the caramel is still runny and the sponge still warm. When making caramel, it is important not to stir the bubbling sugar mixture, otherwise it may crystallise. Instead, move the caramel around in the pan by occasionally tipping the pan very gently from side to side.

200g butter, softened, plus extra for greasing

55g light soft brown sugar

4 tbsp maple syrup

3 small bananas, each cut into three lengthways

150g caster sugar

3 large eggs

½ tsp vanilla extract

155g plain flour

1 tsp baking powder

Pinch of sea salt

Clotted or double cream, crème fraîche or vanilla ice cream, to serve

1. Preheat the oven to 180°C/160°C fan/Gas 4. Grease and line the base of a non-stick, deep round cake tin, measuring 20cm diameter x 6–7cm deep, with baking parchment (make sure you use a tin with a fixed base; don't use a loose-based one).

2. To make the caramel, place 50g of the butter, the brown sugar and maple syrup in a heavy-based saucepan. Cook over a medium heat for 4–5 minutes, stirring initially until the sugar has dissolved, then raise the heat slightly so the mixture is bubbling and keep cooking (without stirring) for a further 4–5 minutes, until the caramel is rich and golden.

3. Remove from the heat and let the bubbles subside slightly, then pour the caramel evenly into the prepared tin to cover the base completely, quickly spreading it if necessary. Arrange the bananas, cut side down, in a single layer over the caramel, trimming the last piece to fit if necessary (you may have a slice left over).

4. To make the cake, place the remaining 150g of butter and the caster sugar in a mixing bowl and beat together until pale and creamy. Add the eggs, one at a time, beating well after each addition, then add the vanilla extract. Sift the flour, baking powder and salt together, and then gently fold into the creamed mixture, half at a time. Spoon this mixture over the bananas and caramel, spreading evenly with a spatula.

5. Bake for about 1 hour, checking after 50 minutes to make sure the top is not browning too quickly (if it is, lay a loose piece of foil over the top). When done, the cake should be risen and golden brown, and a skewer inserted into the centre should come out clean; if not, return the cake to the oven for a further 5 minutes.

6. Cool in the tin for 5 minutes, then loosen the sides with a small knife and carefully invert the cake onto a serving plate with a rim (to catch any caramel). Cut into wedges and serve warm with clotted or double cream, crème fraîche or vanilla ice cream.

# BSK rum punch

There's nothing like a bowl of rum punch to get a party started. Our special combination of four different types of rum mixed with lime juice, cold Earl Grey tea, cinnamon syrup, pineapple purée and star anise, is both refreshing and spicy at the same time. Finished off with tangy grapefruit segments, one glass will transport you to the Caribbean.

1. Put all the ingredients into a jug with some ice cubes and stir until ice cold.

2. Pour into 5 glasses to serve.

SERVES 5

100ml white rum

50ml aged rum

50ml spiced rum

50ml Demerara rum

125ml fresh lime juice

100ml brewed Earl Grey tea, cooled

70ml cinnamon syrup (see Tip)

100ml pineapple purée (see Tip)

1 grapefruit, segmented

5 star anise

Ice cubes

TIP

You can buy cinnamon syrup for coffees and cocktails online; likewise, you can buy pineapple purée online too.

# Vodka, lime and elderflower pressé

What better way to greet guests at an al fresco lunch party than with a big jug of a delicious summery cocktail like this one? The combination of vodka, lime, apple and elderflower is so refreshing and quaffable that it should come with a warning – this drink does contain alcohol!

1. Put the vodka, lime juice, apple juice and elderflower cordial into a jug or cocktail shaker with a large handful of ice cubes, and mix together thoroughly.

2. Divide among 4 tall glasses and top up with soda water.

3. Put a slice of apple and a strip of lime zest into each glass and sprinkle with the chopped herbs to garnish. Serve.

SERVES 4

200ml vodka

100ml fresh lime juice

100ml freshly pressed apple juice

60ml elderflower cordial

Ice cubes

Soda water

*To garnish*

4 slices of dessert apple, such as Granny Smith

4 strips of pared lime zest

Little chopped fresh basil and chopped fresh mint, for sprinkling

# IN BETWEEN MEALS

Bread Street Kitchen is never empty; during the day there are, of course, much quieter periods but it is never completely deserted. People come in at elevenish for a brownie and a cappuccino, groups of City workers hold meetings out of the office, shoppers stop for a cup of tea and a sit down in the afternoon, then nine-to-fivers arrive for cocktails after work. Because the kitchen is open all day, we always have something to offer people, whatever time they come in.

Obviously, this isn't the case at home but it's nice to feel that you're prepared for the gaps between meals with a handful of tried-and-tested sweet snacks that work for every occasion. Make brownies to boost your popularity in the office (this really works!), keep cookie dough in the freezer for when friends pop in without warning

(nothing beats the smell of freshly baked biscuits), make mini doughnuts with the kids (they will love you forever) or fill up with a fresh banana smoothie or an iced coffee.

We all know we are supposed to be cutting down on our sugar intake, but if you make your treats from scratch, at least you know that there are no hidden nasties in them and a small slice of home-made Bakewell tart will be infinitely superior to a shop-bought one in every way. The added bonus is the enormous satisfaction and sense of pride you get from baking at home.

Anyway, they say that a little of what you fancy does you good – and we're not going to argue with that.

# IN BETWEEN MEALS

# Fruit and nut biscotti

Biscotti are nutty biscuits that are twice-baked for that characteristic crunchiness. They are traditionally made with almonds, but we use a combination of whole nuts and throw in some sultanas and orange zest too for a fruitier, nuttier version. Delicious served with coffee, they are also amazing dunked into a glass of Vin Santo dessert wine at the end of a meal.

1. Preheat the oven to 180°C/160°C fan/Gas 4. Line a baking sheet with baking parchment.

2. Put the flour, sugar and baking powder into a large bowl and mix together. Add the sultanas, nuts and orange zest, and mix again. Make a well in the middle and pour in the egg. Stir with a spoon until the mixture starts to clump together. Use your hands to bring all the ingredients together, kneading gently to mop up the excess dry ingredients to make a soft dough.

3. Transfer the dough to the prepared baking sheet, then roll and shape it gently until it measures a log about 23 x 5cm in size. Bake the log for 20–25 minutes, until it is golden brown and feels firm when lightly pressed on top.

4. Remove from the oven and cool for 5 minutes on a wire rack, keeping the baking sheet to one side. Reduce the oven temperature to 140°C/120°C fan/Gas 1. Transfer the warm log to a chopping/bread board, then use a large serrated knife to slice it on the diagonal into 16–18 slices, each about 1cm thick. Turn each slice on its side and then lay them all out on the baking sheet.

5. Return the biscuits to the oven and bake for a further 20–25 minutes, turning over halfway through, until golden and crisp. Transfer to a wire rack to cool completely. Store in an airtight container for up to a week.

MAKES 16-18 BISCOTTI

100g plain flour

50g light soft brown sugar

½ tsp baking powder

20g sultanas

20g whole pistachio nuts

20g whole almonds

10g whole hazelnuts

Finely grated zest of ¼ orange

1 egg, beaten

# World's best brownies

Every chef thinks that their brownie recipe is the best, but we think this one really is the crème de la crème. The brownies are excellent when they are still warm from the oven but, should you have any left, they are also really good cold as the warm centre becomes slightly more chewy. Adding chocolate chunks to the half-baked brownie during cooking will give you little pockets of melted chocolate in almost every bite – pure heaven!

1. Preheat the oven to 180°C/160°C fan/Gas 4. Grease and line a 30 x 23cm cake tin with baking parchment.

2. Put the chocolate and butter into a large heatproof bowl set over a pan of gently simmering water (don't let the bottom of the bowl touch the water underneath) and leave until melted, stirring occasionally (see Tip).

3. Remove from the heat and cool down the chocolate by mixing in the sugars using a balloon whisk. Add the eggs and vanilla extract, and mix in with a wooden spoon until combined. Sift over the flour and salt, and stir again until smooth and combined. Pour into the prepared tin, smoothing the top level.

4. Bake for 35–40 minutes, until cracked around the edges and soft in the middle (it will firm up as it cools), rotating the tin halfway through baking.

5. If you are adding the chocolate chunks, take the brownie out of the oven after 20 minutes and vigorously throw the chunks of chocolate at the half-baked brownie so they break the surface. Return to the oven for the remaining cooking time.

6. Transfer the brownie to a wire rack and leave it to cool in the tin, then cut into squares before serving. Once cooled, the brownies will keep in an airtight container for up to a week (see Tip). Alternatively, cool the cooked brownie in the tin for 10 minutes, then cut into squares and serve warm with a dollop of thick cream, if you like.

MAKES 15-20 BROWNIES

245g dark chocolate, broken into squares or roughly chopped

200g butter, diced, plus extra for greasing

175g caster sugar

125g light soft brown sugar

4 large eggs, lightly beaten

2 tsp vanilla extract

115g plain flour

Pinch of sea salt

100g dark chocolate, chopped into small chunks (optional)

Thick cream, to serve (optional)

TIPS

If you prefer, put the chocolate and butter into a heatproof bowl, cover (leaving a small air gap) and melt in the microwave on low for about 3 minutes, stirring and checking every 30 seconds or so.

These brownies also freeze well for up to a month. Simply wrap them tightly in cling film and freeze, then thaw at a cool room temperature before serving.

# Walnut chocolate chip cookies

Adding nuts to chocolate chip cookies makes them that little bit healthier, so you can feel less guilty about having another one… and another. Swap the walnuts for hazelnuts, pistachios or almonds if you prefer, and enjoy these cookies dunked into a hot mug of tea or coffee. Alternatively, roll the raw dough into a log, then wrap it in cling film and keep it in the freezer for when friends turn up unexpectedly; simply unwrap and slice the frozen dough into 1cm rounds, then follow the cooking instructions below, increasing the cooking time a little if the biscuits are still frozen when they go into the oven.

1. Preheat the oven to 200°C/180°C fan/Gas 6. Grease three baking sheets.

2. Put the butter and sugar into a large bowl and cream together until light and fluffy. Mix in the egg, then sift over the flour and salt, and fold in until combined. Stir in the chopped walnuts and chocolate chunks until evenly distributed.

3. Pull off walnut-sized pieces of the dough (see Tip) and roll them roughly into balls between your hands. Place on the prepared baking sheets, about 5cm apart, press down with a fork to flatten. Bake for 8–10 minutes or until lightly golden around the edges and still soft in the middle.

4. Cool slightly on the baking sheets, then using a spatula, transfer the cookies to a wire rack and leave to cool completely before serving. These cookies will keep in an airtight container for up to 5 days (see Tip).

MAKES ABOUT 28 COOKIES

110g butter, softened, plus extra for greasing

180g light soft brown sugar

1 egg, beaten

190g plain flour

Pinch of sea salt

90g walnuts, chopped

180g dark chocolate, chopped into small chunks

TIPS

Use a tablespoon measuring spoon to scoop out the cookie dough, before rolling into a ball.

These cookies also freeze well for up to a month. Simply freeze them in a sealed freezer bag or wrapped tightly in cling film, then thaw at a cool room temperature before serving.

# Rosemary shortbread

Adding rosemary to this fantastic shortbread works really well, but as a variation you could try lemon thyme, finely grated lemon or orange zest, fennel seeds or even dried edible lavender – just take the foolproof base and use your imagination. The base is also very delicious on its own if you prefer a plain shortbread biscuit – just leave the rosemary out. This recipe makes lots of shortbread fingers, but they keep well in a biscuit tin for when you need a sugar boost between meals, or you can easily halve the recipe, if you prefer.

1. Preheat the oven to 170°C/150°C fan/Gas 3. Grease a baking sheet.

2. Sift the flour and salt into a large bowl, then stir in the sugar. Rub in the butter using your fingertips until the mixture resembles fine breadcrumbs. Stir in the chopped rosemary, then knead and squeeze the mixture together with warm hands until it's well combined and smooth (with no wrinkles or cracks).

3. Cut the dough in half and roll out one half on a lightly floured work surface to a 12 x 12cm square, about 1cm thick. Cut into 2cm slices, then cut each slice in half through the middle to make 12 fingers. Prick all over with a fork and transfer to the prepared baking sheet. Repeat with the other piece of dough to make 24 fingers in total.

4. Bake for about 30 minutes, until the shortbread is golden and looks a little risen and spongy.

5. Remove from the oven and sprinkle the shortbread fingers with caster sugar, if you like, then leave to cool completely on the baking sheet. Store in an airtight container for up to 5 days (see Tip).

MAKES 24 SHORTBREADS

225g plain flour, plus extra for dusting

Pinch of sea salt

75g caster sugar, plus extra for sprinkling (optional)

150g butter, at room temperature, cubed, plus extra for greasing

1 small rosemary sprig, leaves picked and finely chopped

TIP
These shortbread fingers also freeze well for up to a month. Simply wrap them tightly in cling film and freeze, then thaw at a cool room temperature before serving.

# Mini doughnuts

Using a pre-ferment or poolish to make these doughnuts is a little more time-consuming than using the direct or straight yeast method, but the resulting texture is lighter and the taste richer. The added bonus is that the finished doughnuts will last a little longer, if they're not all eaten immediately – they are very moreish!

1. To make the poolish, put the flour, lukewarm water, yeast and sugar into a bowl and whisk together to mix. Leave to ferment in a warm place for 15 minutes.

2. For the dough, put the flour into a mixing bowl, then stir in the sugar and salt. Make a well in the middle, then add the egg yolks, poolish, melted butter and yeast and water mixture, and mix well with a table knife to make a soft dough. Transfer to a clean work surface and knead until smooth. This will take about 8–10 minutes. (You can make the dough using a stand mixer fitted with a dough hook, if you prefer.)

3. Transfer the dough to an oiled clean bowl, cover with cling film and leave to rise in a warm place for 1–2 hours or until doubled in size.

4. Oil a tray or board and set aside. Turn out the dough onto a lightly floured surface and knead for a minute or so. Divide the dough into about 20 small pieces, then roll each piece into a small ball. Place the balls on the oiled tray or board, spacing them well apart. Cover with a clean tea towel and leave to rise in a warm place for 45 minutes–1 hour or until doubled in size.

5. Once the balls have risen, heat a deep-fat fryer to 180°C or fill a large saucepan one-third full of vegetable oil and heat until a cube of bread dropped in the oil sizzles and turns golden in 30 seconds.

6. Meanwhile, mix the sugar and cinnamon in a mixing bowl.

7. Deep-fry the doughnuts in the hot oil, a few at a time, for about 5 minutes, turning them over halfway through, until cooked and a lovely golden colour all over.

8. Remove each batch of cooked doughnuts with a slotted spoon, drain on kitchen paper, then put them straight into the bowl of cinnamon sugar, tossing to dredge them with the sugar. Deep-fry the remaining doughnuts in the same way, dredging each batch with cinnamon sugar as soon as they come out of the fryer. Serve them freshly made and warm.

MAKES ABOUT 20 MINI DOUGHNUTS

*For the poolish*
100g plain flour
100ml lukewarm water
1 tsp dried active yeast granules
1 tsp caster sugar

*For the dough*
250g plain flour, plus extra for dusting
60g caster sugar
1 tsp sea salt
3 large egg yolks
20g butter, melted and cooled
1 tsp dried active yeast granules, blended with a little warm water
Vegetable oil, for deep-frying, plus extra for greasing

*For the cinnamon sugar*
75g caster sugar
1 tsp ground cinnamon

# Cherry Bakewell tart

Bakewell tart is a real tea-time favourite. Our version of this British classic replaces the raspberry jam with cherry and has whole fresh cherries inserted into the frangipane for pockets of intense flavour. The pastry dough is extremely soft and can be a little tricky to handle so keep it as cold as possible.

1. Make the pastry. Cream the butter and sugar together in a bowl until light and creamy, then gradually beat in one of the beaten eggs. Gradually stir in the flour and salt, adding a third of the flour at a time, bringing it all together to make a very soft dough. Briefly work into a ball with your hands, but do not overhandle. Pat into a flat round, wrap in cling film and chill in the fridge for about 1 hour before rolling out. If the dough still feels soft, chill it for a bit longer (see Tip).

2. Roll out the pastry on a lightly floured surface and use it to line a 24cm-round, 2.5cm-deep fluted loose-based tart tin, leaving some excess pastry overhanging the rim (reserve any leftover bits of pastry for patching up the base, if needed). Prick the base all over with a fork, then chill in the fridge for 30 minutes.

3. Preheat the oven to 200°C/180°C fan/Gas 6. Place the pastry-lined tin on a baking sheet, line with baking parchment and fill with baking beans or uncooked rice. Bake 'blind' for 15 minutes. Remove from the oven, remove the baking beans and paper, then patch up any cracks in the pastry case with the reserved pastry, if necessary. Brush the remaining beaten egg over the pastry case. Return to the oven for 5 minutes, until the base is cooked and pale golden.

4. Remove from the oven and reduce the oven temperature to 180°C/160°C fan/Gas 4. While still warm, use a sharp knife to trim off the excess pastry level with the rim of the tin, then brush out any loose crumbs from inside the baked case. Leave to cool completely.

5. Cream the butter and sugar together in a bowl until light and fluffy. Gradually beat in the eggs, then stir in the ground almonds, flour and almond extract until combined.

6. Spread the jam over the base of the pastry case, then spoon over the frangipane. Smooth with a palette knife, then press the cherries into the frangipane. Sprinkle with the flaked almonds.

7. Bake the tart for 40 minutes, until set. Remove from the oven, brush the top with the honey, then bake for a further 4–5 minutes, until the honey is set and the tart is glossy, checking that the top doesn't overbrown. Leave to cool completely before removing it from the tin. Slice and serve with clotted cream.

SERVES 8-10

*For the pastry*
125g butter, softened
75g icing sugar, sifted
2 large eggs, beaten separately
250g plain flour, plus extra for dusting
Pinch of sea salt

*For the filling*
150g butter, softened
150g caster sugar
3 large eggs, beaten
150g ground almonds
25g plain flour
1 tsp almond extract
3 tbsp cherry jam
15 fresh cherries, stems removed and stoned
30g flaked almonds
1–2 tbsp runny honey

Clotted cream, to serve

TIP
If you have time, overnight chilling for the raw pastry works best, so that it firms up. Just remove it from the fridge about 30 minutes before rolling out so it is manageable.

# Treacle tart

Everyone loves a really good treacle tart – it's old-fashioned nursery food at its best and always popular at any time of the day. To weigh golden syrup accurately, brush your spoon and measuring bowl with a thin coat of vegetable oil; then the syrup will slip easily into the mixing bowl and you will be sure the full amount makes it into the tart.

SERVES 8-10

*For the pastry*

125g butter, softened

75g icing sugar, sifted

2 large eggs, beaten separately

250g plain flour, plus extra
    for dusting

Pinch of sea salt

*For the filling*

350g golden syrup

85g fresh white breadcrumbs

50g ground almonds

2 large eggs, beaten

100ml double cream

Custard or double or clotted
    cream, to serve

1. Make the pastry. Cream the butter and sugar together in a bowl until light and creamy, then gradually beat in one of the beaten eggs. Gradually stir in the flour and salt, adding a third of the flour at a time, bringing it all together to make a very soft dough. Briefly work into a ball with your hands, but do not overhandle. Pat into a flat round, wrap in cling film and chill in the fridge for about 1 hour before rolling out. If the dough still feels soft, chill it a bit longer.

2. Roll out the pastry on a lightly floured surface and use it to line a 24cm-round, 2.5cm-deep fluted loose-based tart tin, leaving some excess pastry overhanging the rim (reserve any leftover bits of pastry for patching up the base, if needed). Prick the base all over with a fork, then chill in the fridge for 30 minutes.

3. Preheat the oven to 200°C/180°C fan/Gas 6. Place the pastry-lined tin on a baking sheet, line with baking parchment and fill with baking beans or uncooked rice. Bake 'blind' for 15 minutes. Remove from the oven, remove the baking beans and paper, then patch up any cracks in the case with the reserved pastry, if necessary. Brush the remaining beaten egg over the pastry. Return to the oven for 5 minutes, until the base is cooked and pale golden.

4. Remove from the oven and reduce the oven temperature to 180°C/160°C fan/Gas 4. While still warm, use a sharp knife to trim off the excess pastry level with the rim of the tin, then brush out any loose crumbs from inside the case. Leave to cool completely.

5. Put the syrup, breadcrumbs and almonds into a bowl and mix together. Add the eggs and cream, and stir together until well combined. Pour into the baked pastry case and smooth the top.

6. Bake the tart for 30–35 minutes, until golden brown and lightly set.

7. Leave the tart to cool completely before removing it from the tin, then slice and serve with custard or double or clotted cream.

# Honey bee
# banana smoothie

This filling honey and banana smoothie is popular with young kids and not-so-little kids who love a banana milkshake. This version is dairy-free, but you could substitute the almond milk for cow's milk, or instead try soya, rice or oat milk. Sprinkle a little extra granola on top of the glass for extra appeal and crunch. The recipe is easily doubled too, if you have more than one hungry mouth waiting.

1. Chop the banana and place it in a blender with the almond milk, honey and granola. Blitz together until smooth.

2. Pour into a tall glass, sprinkle with granola and drink immediately.

SERVES 1

1 banana

125ml almond milk

1 tbsp runny honey

50g Granola (see page 21), plus extra to serve


# Maple syrup
# iced coffee

Drinking iced coffee is the perfect way to get your coffee fix on hot days. This luxurious version is laced with maple syrup to give it natural sweetness and that distinctive caramel flavour. Drink immediately, or pour it into a flask and take it with you for a great mid-morning pick-me-up.

1. Put all the ingredients into a shaker and gently roll together to chill and slightly dilute the liquid. Over-shaking or shaking too hard will make it watery.

2. Pour into a tall glass, garnish with coffee beans and drink immediately.

SERVES 1

Double shot of hot espresso coffee

125ml whole milk

Small pinch of ground cinnamon

1 tbsp maple syrup

Ice cubes

Coffee beans, to serve

# Try harder

The name for this drink came from the seemingly endless search for the perfect mocktail. Each time the team presented a new mix to the bar manager he sent it back telling them to try harder. This combination of fresh raspberries, plus sweet and sharp fruit juices/ syrup, finished off with sparkling soda water, was the first drink that ticked all the right boxes and it's now the bestselling non-alcoholic drink on the bar menu. If at first you don't succeed…

1. Crush the raspberries in the bottom of a jug or cocktail shaker.

2. Pour in the apple juice, cranberry juice, raspberry syrup and lemon juice, and mix or shake thoroughly.

3. Pour into two tall glasses and top up with soda water.

4. Garnish each glass with a raspberry and a mint sprig before serving.

SERVES 2

10 fresh raspberries,
   plus 2 for the garnish
200ml apple juice
200ml cranberry juice
40ml raspberry syrup
30ml lemon juice
Soda water, to finish
2 mint sprigs, to garnish

# Nice tea

Iced tea is brilliantly thirst-quenching on summer days and brewing it at home is really easy. Make your own peach purée by blitzing a peeled and stoned fresh peach using a stick blender in a bowl, and buy passion fruit syrup online. Make sure you brew the tea until it is nice and strong, as the ice will dilute it as it melts and the flavour will become less intense. Increase the quantities to make a jugful for sharing with a group of friends, and ideally drink it in dappled shade on a sunny afternoon.

1. Pour all the ingredients into a cocktail shaker with ice cubes and shake until thoroughly mixed together and cold.

2. Pour into a tall glass, garnish with the lemon zest and mint sprig, and serve.

SERVES 1

60ml brewed Earl Grey
   tea, cooled
20ml peach purée
25ml lemon juice
15ml passion fruit syrup
Ice cubes

*To garnish*
1 strip of pared lemon zest
1 mint sprig

# MIDWEEK SUPPERS

Possibly the toughest cooking job of all is feeding yourself and your family every day, week after week, all year round. It can be a challenge to come up with new ideas for meals, not to mention finding the time to do the shopping, prepping, cooking and clearing up. It's not surprising that many people rely on ready meals to get through the week, only cooking from scratch at the weekend. But with the right recipes, some clever shopping and good time management, we're confident you can rediscover your midweek mojo.

Here we'll help you refresh your repertoire with a handful of easy-to-achieve recipes; there are quick family-friendly pasta dishes (see page 180 for a pasta sauce so simple it doesn't even need cooking), unfussy but deeply tasty fish suppers and new ways to serve the humble chicken breast. Keep your cupboards and fridge stocked with useful ingredients such as olives, sun-dried tomatoes, capers, garlic, Parmesan and lemons which can pep up your regular dishes or be combined to make sauces and dressings. Use up leftover meat and vegetables in pies, salads and soups and make double batches to create more leftovers for the following day. Use your freezer: next time you cook a crowd-pleasing shepherd's pie at the weekend, double the recipe to make two and put one in the freezer for another night when you have less time. The same goes for the meatballs and the spinach and ricotta cannelloni, which both freeze beautifully for up to a month.

Trying new recipes will put the pleasure back into midweek meals and, though you might have to succumb to the odd ready meal or takeaway every now and again, real cooking won't just be something you only do at the weekend.

# MIDWEEK SUPPERS

# Eggs piperade

Eggs piperade is a rich and satisfying baked egg dish from the Basque region of south west France. Pleasingly, it is cooked in just one frying pan so there is less washing up, too. Don't cook the eggs for too long though because they will continue to cook once you take the pan off the heat – the yolks should be runny when you cut into them.

1. First reduce the beef stock. Pour it into a large saucepan and bring to the boil, then boil, uncovered, over a medium–high heat for about 30 minutes, until reduced by half – you need 500ml of reduced stock for this recipe. Set aside.

2. Meanwhile, heat 2 teaspoons of the oil in a large, deep frying pan or sauté pan over a medium heat, then add the chorizo or pancetta (if using Parma ham, you'll add this later) and sauté for 4–6 minutes, until starting to become crisp. Remove with a slotted spoon and set aside to drain on kitchen paper.

3. Leave 1 tablespoon of the chorizo/pancetta oil in the pan, drain off the rest, then add 1 tablespoon of olive oil to the pan (if using Parma ham, add 2 tablespoons of fresh olive oil to the pan). Heat the oil, then tip in the onions, garlic and thyme and cook over a medium heat, stirring occasionally, until the onions are softened and reduced down, about 10–12 minutes. Add another 1–2 teaspoons of oil during cooking, if needed.

4. Pour in the wine and bubble over a medium–high heat for 2–3 minutes, until it has almost all disappeared, then add the reduced beef stock and the tomato purée and bubble until reduced by at least half, 12–15 minutes. It should be like a thickish onion gravy.

5. Reduce the heat, stir in the peppers, cream (if using) and the reserved chorizo or pancetta and simmer for 5 minutes. Stir in the Parma ham (if using) at this stage to warm through. Remove the thyme stalks, and stir in the flat leaf parsley, then season the sauce to taste with salt and pepper, if needed (see Tip).

6. Make four indents in the sauce, then crack an egg into each one (if you crack each egg into a cup first, you can slide it in and control its shape better). Put a lid on the pan and cook over a low–medium heat with the onion mixture simmering gently around the eggs for about 5 minutes, until the eggs are cooked to your liking. Sprinkle a pinch of paprika over the eggs then spoon into bowls and serve with the sourdough.

SERVES 4

1 litre good-quality beef stock

2–3 tbsp olive oil

225g cooking chorizo, pancetta or Parma ham, diced or chopped

3 red onions, thinly sliced

2 garlic cloves, crushed

4 thyme sprigs

150ml red wine

1 tbsp tomato purée

6 piquillo peppers, (from a jar), sliced

50ml double cream (optional)

1 tbsp chopped flat leaf parsley

4 large eggs

Sea salt and freshly ground black pepper

Pinch of smoked paprika

4 slices of sourdough bread, to serve

TIP
The sauce can be made a day ahead, then cooled and stored in an airtight container in the fridge. Simply reheat it the next day, then crack in the eggs and cook as above.

# Spaghetti crudaiola

*Crudo* is the Italian word for raw and this quick and easy pasta sauce requires no cooking at all. Perfect for a summer's evening, it is wonderfully fresh and light, but make sure you use really ripe tomatoes – the success of the sauce relies on the flavour and sweetness of the tomatoes. Always save a little of the cooking water when draining pasta as it helps to bind the sauce to the pasta.

1. Cook the spaghetti in a large pan of boiling salted water for 11 minutes or until al dente, according to the packet instructions, stirring occasionally.

2. While the pasta is cooking, crush the capers with the anchovies to create a chunky paste (a pestle and mortar is ideal for doing this). Gently crush all the tomatoes in a bowl, squeezing them by hand to release the juices. Add the caper and anchovy paste, the olive oil, garlic, olives and chopped basil, and stir to mix.

3. Drain the spaghetti in a large colander, reserving 2 tablespoons of the pasta water. Stir the reserved water into the tomato mixture. Tip the pasta into a serving bowl, add the sauce and stir it through to mix. Season with pepper to taste (but no salt, as the anchovies and olives are salty).

4. Serve in warmed bowls or on plates, sprinkled with a cheese of your choice, and garnish with basil leaves. Serve warm or at room temperature.

SERVES 4
*(or 6 for a light lunch)*

400g dried spaghetti

15g capers, drained weight

30–40g anchovies in olive oil, drained weight

250g cherry tomatoes (preferably datterini), sliced

200g plum tomatoes (preferably bull's heart), diced

125ml extra virgin olive oil

1 garlic clove, finely chopped

50g pitted black olives

6 fresh basil leaves, chopped, plus extra to garnish

Sea salt and freshly ground black pepper

Dry ricotta, crumbled feta or grated Parmesan cheese, to serve

# Spinach, ricotta and artichoke cannelloni

Spinach and ricotta cannelloni is a much-loved Italian restaurant classic. We add artichokes to ours, which works brilliantly and adds extra texture. You can fill the cannelloni tubes with a teaspoon, but using a piping bag is much quicker and less fiddly. Or, if you don't have a piping bag, spoon the filling mixture into a freezer bag instead, then cut off one bottom corner and pipe away – it works just as well.

1. Preheat the oven to 200°C/180°C fan/Gas 6.

2. Make the cheese sauce. Pour the milk and cream into a saucepan, then heat gently until warm. Melt the butter in a separate saucepan over a low heat, then stir in the flour to make a roux and cook for 1 minute, stirring. Gradually whisk in the warm milk and cream mixture, until the mixture is smooth. Slowly bring to the boil over a low heat, whisking continuously, until the sauce thickens. Simmer gently for 2 minutes, stirring often. Remove from the heat, stir in the mustard, then add the cheese and whisk in until smooth. Season to taste with salt.

3. Meanwhile, for the cannelloni, put the spinach into a large heatproof bowl. Pour over boiling water to cover and leave for 30 seconds, just until wilted. Immediately drain and cool quickly under running cold water. Squeeze out any excess water, then pat dry on kitchen paper and roughly chop the spinach.

4. Put the ricotta, mascarpone and Parmesan into a bowl with the artichokes, egg yolk and blanched spinach, and mix together until well combined. Season with the grated nutmeg and a little salt. Transfer the mixture to a piping bag fitted with a large plain nozzle, then pipe the mix into the cannelloni tubes, dividing it evenly.

5. Lay the filled tubes in an ovenproof dish in a single layer. Pour over the cheese sauce, then sprinkle with the grated Cheddar. Bake for 20 minutes, then increase the oven temperature to 220°C/200°C fan/Gas 7 and bake for a further 10 minutes, until the top is golden and crisp. Serve immediately with a green salad.

SERVES 4

*For the cheese sauce*
280ml whole milk
140ml double cream
25g butter
25g plain flour
½ tsp Dijon mustard
50g mature Cheddar cheese, finely grated
Sea salt

*For the stuffed cannelloni*
260g spinach, rinsed
250g ricotta cheese
80g mascarpone
30g Parmesan cheese, grated
2 tinned (or jarred) artichoke hearts, drained and roughly chopped
1 egg yolk
½ tsp freshly grated nutmeg
8 dried cannelloni tubes
150g mature Cheddar cheese, grated (or use half Cheddar and half mozzarella, if you like it stringy)

# Mac and cheese

The mixture of four cheeses in our mac and cheese is what makes it so deeply satisfying. Comté, Cheddar, mozzarella and Parmesan come together to make an intensely rich sauce for the macaroni, then the garlicky, crispy crumbs give it an exceptionally delicious crunchy top – we defy you not to go back for seconds!

1. Pour the milk into a saucepan, then add the onion, garlic cloves, bay leaf and star anise. Bring almost to the boil, then remove from the heat, cover and set aside to infuse for 30 minutes. Strain into a jug and discard the flavourings.

2. Preheat the oven to 200°C/180°C fan/Gas 6.

3. Melt the butter in a separate large saucepan over a low heat, then stir in the flour to make a roux and cook for 1 minute, stirring. Gradually whisk in the warm infused milk, until the mixture is smooth. Slowly bring to the boil over a low heat, whisking continuously, until the sauce thickens. Simmer gently for 5 minutes, stirring often. Remove from the heat, add the Comté and Cheddar cheeses, and whisk in until smooth. Season to taste with salt and pepper.

4. In the meantime, cook the macaroni in a large pan of salted boiling water until al dente, about 9 minutes, or according to the packet instructions. Drain, refresh briefly under cold running water and drain again.

5. Meanwhile, make the breadcrumb topping. Melt the butter in a frying pan, add the garlic and sauté for a minute without colouring. Stir in the breadcrumbs and cook over a low heat for about 8 minutes, until the breadcrumbs are pale golden and lightly toasted, stirring regularly to make sure the mixture doesn't burn. Stir in the parsley.

6. Tip the macaroni into the cheese sauce and mix well to coat. Pour the mixture into a large, wide gratin dish. Scatter the mozzarella on top, then sprinkle over the Parmesan. Sprinkle the toasted breadcrumbs over the top.

7. Bake for 15–20 minutes, until the topping is golden and crisp. Serve immediately with a crisp salad.

SERVES 6-8

1.3 litres whole milk

¼ onion

2 garlic cloves, peeled and left whole

1 bay leaf

1 star anise

100g butter

100g plain flour

100g Comté cheese, grated

100g mature Cheddar cheese, grated

500g dried macaroni

2 x 150g mozzarella balls, drained and sliced or torn into pieces

30g Parmesan, grated

Sea salt and freshly ground black pepper

*For the breadcrumb topping*

25g butter

2 garlic cloves, crushed

100g fresh white breadcrumbs

4 tbsp finely chopped fresh flat leaf parsley

# Lemon sole
## *with fresh peas*

Lemon sole is a flat fish that has delicate flesh and a mild flavour and it goes wonderfully well with these basil-scented garden peas. Get your fishmonger to remove the fish heads and dark skin for you, which can be quite thick. The lemony breadcrumbs add a lovely crunch and the chilli flakes give a mild heat, but if time is pressing, you can leave them out.

1. First make the toasted-breadcrumb garnish. Mix the breadcrumbs with the olive oil in a small bowl, then transfer to a small frying pan and toast over a medium heat for a few minutes, until evenly golden, stirring often so they don't burn. Remove from the heat and stir in the lemon zest and chilli flakes. Set aside.

2. Put the butter, spring onions, peas, basil, vegetable stock or water and a drizzle of olive oil into a small saucepan and season with salt. Cover, bring to the boil over a medium heat, then simmer for 3 minutes.

3. Meanwhile, pat the fish dry with kitchen paper. Dust the fish with a light coating of flour, patting off any excess, and season with salt. Heat a little olive oil in a large, non-stick frying pan, then add the fish and cook over a medium–high heat for 3 minutes on each side, until cooked through.

4. Transfer the lemon sole to serving plates, then, using a slotted spoon, cover with the peas and spring onions. Spoon over some of the buttery juices and sprinkle over the toasted-breadcrumb garnish. Serve each portion with lemon slices on the side and crushed or sautéed new potatoes.

SERVES 2

40g butter

6 spring onions, trimmed and sliced

100g fresh podded peas (you will need about 250g peas in their pods, or use frozen out of season)

Small handful of fresh basil leaves, roughly chopped

100ml vegetable stock or water

1–2 tbsp olive oil

Sea salt

2 whole lemon sole on the bone, about 250g each, dark skin removed (ask your fishmonger to do this, if you prefer), trimmed and washed

1 tbsp plain flour

Lemon slices, to garnish

*For the toasted-breadcrumb garnish*

2 tbsp fresh white breadcrumbs (see Tip)

1 tsp olive oil

¼ tsp finely grated lemon zest

Pinch of dried chilli flakes

TIP
Remove the crusts from 1 small slice of white bread and blend in a food processor to make 2 tablespoons of breadcrumbs.

# Steamed sea bream

*with leeks and brown shrimps*

This simple, elegant fish dish is really easy to pull off in the middle of a busy week. Once you have all the ingredients prepared, just get cooking and a delicious supper will be on the table in next to no time. Steaming is a really delicate way to cook fish and keeps the flesh lovely and moist. Samphire is a sea vegetable that grows in salt marshes around the coast; it is increasingly available in supermarkets, but if you can't find it, just leave it out.

1. Heat the olive oil in a large pan with 4 tablespoons of water, then add the leeks, and cover and cook over a low heat, stirring occasionally, until softened, about 8 minutes. Stir in the garlic and rosemary, season well with salt and pepper, and cook, uncovered, for a further 2–3 minutes.

2. Meanwhile, bring a saucepan of water to the boil, then reduce to a simmer. Place the bream fillets in a tiered steamer over the simmering water for 4 minutes, until cooked through.

3. In the meantime, melt the butter in a separate saucepan and cook over a medium heat, until it becomes a deep nut-brown colour, 2–3 minutes. Squeeze in the lemon juice, then add the samphire, brown shrimps and tomato quarters, and heat gently for a few minutes, until warmed through.

4. Divide the leeks among serving plates, then place the fish fillets on top. Spoon the samphire and shrimp mixture over the top and serve immediately with steamed new potatoes.

SERVES 4

2 tbsp olive oil

2 large leeks, trimmed and finely sliced

1 garlic clove, crushed

1 rosemary sprig, leaves picked and chopped

4 sea bream fillets, about 150–170g each

40g butter

Juice of ½ lemon

100g samphire, rinsed

100g brown shrimps

8 cherry tomatoes, quartered

Sea salt and freshly ground black pepper

# Pan-fried halibut

*with braised chard, potatoes and anchovies*

Halibut is a firm, meaty fish like cod, turbot or haddock, with a mild taste that can stand up to relatively strong flavours. We pair it with delicious braised potatoes, chard and anchovies for a cracking kitchen supper that is sure to delight. Halibut has a tendency to dry out, so adding a little butter and fish stock during the cooking will keep it moist.

1. Melt 25g of the butter in a large saucepan or sauté pan, then add the shallots and garlic, and cook over a medium heat, stirring constantly, until soft but not coloured, 7–8 minutes. Add the potatoes and cook, stirring, for a further 2 minutes.

2. Stir in the anchovies, Noilly Prat and 500ml of the fish stock. Bring to the boil, then cover, reduce the heat and simmer until the potatoes are tender, about 12 minutes. When the potatoes are almost cooked, stir in the chard, season to taste with salt and pepper, then cover and continue to cook for about 4–5 minutes, until the chard is wilted and just done, but not losing its colour.

3. Meanwhile, season the halibut with salt. Heat the vegetable oil in a large frying pan, add the fish fillets and pan-fry over a medium–high heat for about 3 minutes, until pale golden underneath. Turn the fillets over and cook for 30 seconds, then add remaining butter and the remaining fish stock, whisking gently around the fish to make an emulsion. Reduce the heat and cook for a further 1–2 minutes. Check to see if the fish is cooked using a cocktail stick or skewer – if it goes into the fish easily it is cooked, if not, fry for a little longer.

4. Add the lemon juice and parsley to the pan. Transfer the fish fillets to a serving platter, spoon the pan juices over the whole dish and finish with the chervil (if using). Serve with the braised potatoes, chard and anchovies, serving them from the pan using a slotted spoon and pouring over a spoonful or so of the stock if you like (discard any leftover stock).

SERVES 4

50g butter

3 shallots, finely chopped

3 garlic cloves, finely chopped

1kg potatoes (preferably Desirée or Maris Piper), peeled and sliced

10 anchovies in salt, chopped

100ml Noilly Prat or similar dry vermouth

600ml good-quality fish stock

125g rainbow chard, stems sliced and leaves chopped

4 halibut fillets, about 140–160g each, skin removed

1 tbsp vegetable oil

Squeeze of lemon juice

1 tbsp chopped fresh flat leaf parsley

1 tbsp chopped fresh chervil (optional)

Sea salt and freshly ground black pepper

# Bang bang chicken salad

This Asian-style salad is light but really tasty and is a great way to use up leftover cooked chicken or even turkey after Christmas. As the name implies, it packs a bit of a punch, so leave out the hot stuff if you are cooking for children or non chilli-lovers.

1. For the salad, toast the peanuts in a dry frying pan over a medium heat for a few minutes, shaking the pan occasionally, until golden. Tip into a small bowl.

2. Mix the beansprouts, watercress, radishes, mooli/daikon (if using), chilli and ginger together in a large bowl and season with salt. Stir through half of the toasted peanuts, then dress with the olive oil, tossing to mix everything together. Divide the salad among four bowls.

3. For the chicken, using a pestle and mortar, pound the chilli and garlic together to make a paste. Put the paste and all the remaining ingredients, except the chicken, in a saucepan and mix together until combined. Stir through the chicken until coated. Cook over a medium heat, stirring occasionally, until warmed through, about 2–3 minutes.

4. Spoon the chicken and sauce on top of the salad. Sprinkle over the spring onions and torn coriander, then finish with the remaining toasted peanuts to serve.

SERVES 4

*For the salad*

60g unsalted peanuts, roughly chopped

140g beansprouts

100g watercress

80g breakfast radishes, finely sliced

60g mooli/daikon (Japanese radish), finely sliced (optional)

½–1 red chilli, deseeded and cut into julienne

1 thumb-sized piece of fresh root ginger, peeled and cut into julienne

Sea salt

1 tbsp olive oil

4 spring onions, trimmed and finely sliced, to garnish

Small handful of fresh coriander, torn, to garnish

*For the chicken*

½–1 red chilli, deseeded and quartered

1 garlic clove, peeled

60g peanut butter

2 tsp sesame oil

2 tsp mirin rice wine

2 tsp rice wine vinegar

Pinch of caster sugar

Pinch of paprika

600g cooked chicken breast or thigh, shredded (see Tip)

TIP
If you don't have leftover chicken, poach 4 large skinless, boneless chicken breasts (800g total raw weight) in simmering chicken stock or water for 15–20 minutes, until cooked through. Remove, set aside to cool, then shred the meat.

# Butterflied chicken breasts

*with tomato and olive salsa*

Butterflying chicken breasts (slicing them almost in half horizontally and opening them out like a book, then flattening) helps them to cook more evenly so there is less chance of the meat drying out. It also means that the cooking time is reduced, so supper is on the table that bit faster. The tomato and olive dressing can be prepared the night before to save even more time when you come to cook the chicken the next day.

1. Make the salsa. Put the sunblush or slow-roasted tomatoes, cherry tomatoes, olives and garlic into a bowl and mix together. Set aside 2 teaspoons of the oil, then pour the remaining oil into the bowl, add the oregano and parsley, and stir together until combined. You can do this the day before, if you like, then simply cover and store in the fridge overnight.

2. Cook the green beans in a pan of boiling salted water for 5–6 minutes, until tender, then drain and keep warm.

3. Meanwhile, brush the reserved oil over the butterflied chicken breasts, then season with salt and pepper. Preheat a large griddle pan until hot, then add the chicken breasts and cook over a medium heat for 2–3 minutes on each side, until golden and cooked through. You may need to do this in two batches, depending on the size of your pan.

4. Divide the green beans among serving plates, then place the chicken breasts on top. Spoon a good amount of the salsa over the chicken, then scatter a handful of rocket on top of each portion. Finish with the Parmesan and serve.

SERVES 4

40g sunblush or slow-roasted tomatoes, roughly chopped

20 cherry tomatoes, roughly chopped

20 pitted black olives (such as Kalamata), roughly chopped

1 garlic clove, finely chopped

100ml extra virgin olive oil

1 tsp dried oregano

1 tbsp chopped fresh parsley

250g green beans, trimmed

4 chicken breasts (preferably corn-fed), about 150g each, butterflied (see Tip)

4 handfuls of rocket

10g Parmesan cheese, grated or shaved

Sea salt and freshly ground black pepper

TIP

To butterfly a chicken breast, place the breast on a chopping board and, using a very sharp knife, slice almost all the way through it horizontally – it should remain joined down one side. Then open it like a book, cover with cling film and flatten with a rolling pin until uniformly thin.

# Meatballs

## *with tomato sauce*

There is something very therapeutic about making meatballs and if you prepare them from scratch you know exactly what has gone into them – and in this case, that's only good things. The combination of beef and pork mince is typically Italian, as is serving the cooked meatballs with bread rather than pasta – spaghetti and meatballs is an American invention and our Italian sous chef wouldn't hear of it!

1. First prepare the tomato sauce. Heat the olive oil in a large casserole or heavy-based saucepan, add the onion and cook gently for about 10 minutes, stirring occasionally, until softened but not coloured. Stir in the garlic and cook for a couple more minutes.

2. Pour in the passata and chopped tomatoes along with a good pinch of salt and pepper. Bring to the boil, then simmer, uncovered, over a medium heat for 30 minutes, stirring regularly to make sure the mixture doesn't catch on the bottom.

3. Meanwhile, prepare the meatballs. Preheat the oven to 200°C/180°C fan/Gas 6. Line a large baking tray with baking parchment.

4. Put all the ingredients for the meatballs, except the breadcrumbs and oil, into a large bowl and mix together until well combined, adding the breadcrumbs last. Divide and roll the mixture into small walnut-sized balls, about 30g each (you'll make about 40 meatballs). Place the meatballs on the prepared baking tray in a single layer, then brush all over with the olive oil. Cook in the oven for 10 minutes, until browned.

5. Remove from the oven, then carefully drop the meatballs into the hot tomato sauce in the casserole or saucepan. Cover with the lid and braise over a low heat for 30–45 minutes, stirring a couple of times (making sure that you don't break the meatballs when you stir), until the sauce has thickened and the meatballs are cooked through.

6. Top with basil and Parmesan and serve hot with some fresh crusty bread.

SERVES 4-6

*For the tomato sauce*
2 tbsp olive oil
1 onion, finely chopped
2 garlic cloves, finely chopped
1 litre passata
1 x 400g tin good-quality chopped tomatoes
Sea salt and freshly ground black pepper

*For the meatballs*
800g minced beef, preferably chuck or something not too lean
200g minced pork
2 garlic cloves, finely chopped
4 tbsp whole milk
1 egg
4 thyme sprigs, leaves picked and chopped (or use 1 tsp dried thyme)
4 oregano sprigs, leaves picked and chopped (or use 1 tsp dried oregano)
4 marjoram sprigs, leaves picked and chopped (or use 1 tsp dried marjoram)
4 flat leaf parsley sprigs, leaves picked and chopped
100g fresh white breadcrumbs or crumbs from a stale loaf of bread
3 tbsp olive oil
Handful of basil leaves, torn, to serve
25g shaved Parmesan, to serve

# Shepherd's pie

Everybody loves a good shepherd's pie, whether young or old, and it makes a brilliant family meal. This is great for making ahead as it keeps really well and the flavours improve with time. It also freezes beautifully (before the final bake) for up to a month or so; just thaw it overnight in the fridge and follow the final baking instructions below. The cream in the mashed potato makes it wonderfully velvety and decadent, but you can replace it with whole milk, if you prefer.

1. Heat 1 tablespoon of the vegetable oil in a large saucepan over a high heat, then add half of the diced lamb and cook, stirring regularly, until well coloured all over, about 5 minutes. Remove to a plate. Repeat with the remaining oil and diced lamb, then remove to the plate.

2. Add the onions, 1 carrot, the celery and garlic to the saucepan, then reduce the heat and cook, stirring occasionally, until well coloured, about 10 minutes. Stir in the tomato purée and cook for 3–4 minutes.

3. Add the browned meat to the pan, then pour in the stock and add the herbs. Bring gently to the boil, then cook, uncovered, over a low heat for 1½–2 hours, stirring occasionally, until the sauce has reduced and thickened.

4. Meanwhile, cook the potatoes for the mash in a large pan of salted boiling water, until tender, 15–20 minutes. Drain well, then pass through a potato ricer or mouli, or mash by hand until smooth.

5. Pour the cream into a separate pan and bring gently to the boil, then bubble over a low–medium heat until reduced by half, about 10 minutes. Add the reduced cream and the butter to the mashed potatoes and mix well, then beat in the egg yolks until smooth and combined. Season to taste with salt and pepper.

6. Preheat the oven to 200°C/180°C fan/Gas 6.

7. Melt the butter in a frying pan over a low–medium heat, then add the turnips, the baby onions and remaining carrots, and sauté for 10 minutes, until soft. Stir this mixture into the cooked meat. Add a splash of Worcestershire sauce, then cook, uncovered, over a low heat, stirring regularly, until the mixture is thick, about 5 minutes. Remove the herb stalks, stir in the peas, then pour the lamb mixture into a baking or gratin dish with a capacity of 3–4 litres.

8. Spoon the mashed potato into a piping bag fitted with a star nozzle (if you want a fancy finish) and pipe on top of the meat mixture, covering it completely, or simply spoon over the mash roughly for a more rustic look and run a fork over the top.

9. Place the pie on a baking tray and cook in the oven for 25–30 minutes, until golden brown on top.

SERVES 4-6

*For the meat*

2 tbsp vegetable oil

1kg diced lamb neck

2 onions, chopped

3 large carrots, peeled and diced

2 celery sticks, trimmed and diced

2 garlic cloves, crushed

3 tbsp tomato purée

1 litre beef stock

2 rosemary sprigs

4 thyme sprigs

25g butter

2 large turnips, peeled and diced

4 baby onions, halved

Splash of Worcestershire sauce

300g frozen or fresh (podded weight) peas

*For the mash*

1kg King Edward, Desirée or other red-skinned potatoes, peeled and diced

300ml double cream (see Tip)

50g butter

3 large egg yolks

Sea salt and freshly ground black pepper

TIP
For the mash, you can use 300ml whole milk, or 150ml double cream and 150ml whole milk combined, in place of the cream, if you prefer.

# Beef tagliata

*Tagliare* means to slice in Italian, which is how this sliced beef salad got its name. Traditionally the slices of rare beef are served with rocket and Parmesan, but in this version the steaks rest on a bed of griddled courgette and aubergine ribbons and are topped with a tasty combination of toasted pine nuts, semi-dried tomatoes, fresh basil, balsamic vinegar and a drizzle of olive oil, for a lovely taste of the Mediterranean.

1. Melt the butter in a frying pan, add the pine nuts with a pinch of salt and cook over a low–medium heat for about 3 minutes, stirring regularly, until they are nicely browned and toasted. Remove from the heat and leave to cool.

2. Meanwhile, preheat a griddle pan over a high heat. Add the courgette and aubergine slices to the hot pan in batches (without oil) and cook until they are soft, have griddle marks on them and are slightly charred but not burnt, turning once. Remove the cooked slices to a plate or bowl, drizzle with the olive oil, then sprinkle with the oregano. Set aside and keep warm while you cook the steaks.

3. Rub the steaks with a little olive oil and season both sides with salt. Griddle the steaks in the hot pan for 4–5 minutes on each side, or for longer if you prefer your steak well done. Remove from the griddle pan to a plate and leave to rest for 5 minutes.

4. Toss the griddled vegetables with the pine nuts, tomatoes and basil and divide among serving plates. Slice the steaks and place on top of the vegetables. Drizzle with balsamic vinegar and oil, season with pepper. Scatter with Parmesan before serving.

SERVES 4

25g butter

25g pine nuts

2 courgettes, very finely sliced with a vegetable peeler or mandolin

1 aubergine, very finely sliced with a vegetable peeler or mandolin

2 tbsp extra virgin olive oil, plus extra for drizzling

2 tbsp fresh oregano, torn, or use 1 tbsp dried

4 aged sirloin steaks, about 130g each, at room temperature

20 semi-dried tomatoes

10g fresh basil leaves, torn

1 tbsp aged balsamic vinegar

Sea salt and freshly ground black pepper

40g Parmesan, shaved

# Lamb rump
## *with pea purée and griddled asparagus*

The best way to celebrate the arrival of lamb in the spring is to serve it with other ingredients that come into season at the same time, in this case, Jersey Royal potatoes, asparagus and peas. You could use fresh peas for the purée, but as frozen peas are frozen within hours of being picked, they are considered just as fresh if not fresher than unfrozen ones.

1. Preheat the oven to 200°C/180°C fan/Gas 6. Season the lamb rumps with a little salt. Heat the olive oil in an ovenproof frying pan over a high heat until very hot, then brown the rumps for 2–3 minutes on each side, until well caramelised.

2. Transfer the pan to the oven and roast for 8–10 minutes, until the lamb is cooked but still pink in the centre (or cook for 15–20 minutes, if you prefer well done). Remove from the oven and leave to rest for at least 5 minutes before carving into slices. Keep warm.

3. Meanwhile, make the pea purée. Put the spinach into a large heatproof bowl. Pour boiling water over to cover and leave for 30 seconds, just until wilted. Immediately drain and cool quickly under running cold water. Squeeze out any excess water, then pat dry on kitchen paper and roughly chop the spinach.

4. Put the peas into a saucepan, pour over the hot stock and simmer until tender, 3–4 minutes. Drain well, reserving 100ml of the stock, then blitz the peas and reserved stock in a blender or food processor with the spinach, mint and butter, to make a purée. Season to taste with salt and pepper (you may not need salt as the stock is quite salty). Keep warm.

5. While the peas are cooking, blanch the asparagus in a separate large pan of boiling water for 2–3 minutes, until just tender. Drain, immediately refresh in cold water, then drain again well and pat dry on kitchen paper.

6. Heat a griddle pan until it's very hot and then drizzle in the vegetable oil. Add the blanched asparagus to the pan (you may need to do this in a couple of batches, depending on the size of your pan) and cook over a high heat for 2–3 minutes, turning once, until charred all over.

7. To serve, put a spoonful of the pea purée onto each plate, then sit the lamb slices on top and drizzle with beef jus. Arrange the griddled asparagus alongside, then serve with crushed minted Jersey Royal (or other) new potatoes.

SERVES 4

4 lamb rumps, about 200g each

1 tbsp olive oil

300g spinach, rinsed

500g frozen peas

250ml hot vegetable stock

2 mint sprigs, leaves picked

25g butter

500g asparagus spears, trimmed

1 tbsp vegetable oil

Sea salt and freshly ground black pepper

Beef jus (see page 234), to serve (optional)

# DINNER
# WITH
# FRIENDS

Eating out is one of life's great pleasures, but for many people so is entertaining at home; it gives them the incentive to raise their game in the kitchen, to try new recipes and attempt to impress their friends. But when you go out to a restaurant for dinner, a team of chefs have been peeling, chopping, marinating, basting, baking, sautéing and seasoning all day to produce the meal you will eat. Different sections in the kitchen prepare different components of the dish and they are brought together on the plate under the watchful eye of the head chef before being sent to your table. This is why restaurant food tastes so good.

We know you don't have a brigade of chefs at home and there is a limit to what a domestic cook, even one with plenty of time and skill, can pull off on their own. But we don't see why elements of what we do in the kitchen can't be incorporated into your cooking to make it a little bit more special.

Whether it's reducing sauces, combining unusual and exciting flavours or being brave with new ingredients, we want to inject a bit of professional magic into your kitchen. For example, serving a simple piece of pan-fried hake with unexpected black pudding and a sophisticated, restaurant-quality white wine sauce. Or garnishing fragrant honey panna cotta with dill and elderflower-infused cucumber. These little BSK twists make all the difference.

But impressive doesn't have to mean complicated and there are plenty of ways to make entertaining easier, such as serving a cold starter that requires no last-minute cooking, making one-pot main courses that are cooked low and slow for minimum effort and maximum flavour, or buying in dessert so you only have to make two courses from scratch. You might not need that brigade of chefs after all…

# DINNER WITH FRIENDS

Spicy tuna tartare                                          211
*with wonton crisps*

Stone bass carpaccio                                        212

Pan-fried scallops                                          215
*with Jerusalem artichoke purée,*
*apple and crispy chicken skin*

Roast beef carpaccio                                        216
*with truffle dressing*

Pan-fried cod                                               219
*with artichokes and crushed potatoes*

Pan-fried hake                                              220
*with black pudding and white wine sauce*

Sea trout                                                   223
*with clams*

Chicken ballotines                                          224
*with potato wedges and spicy broccoli*

Pan-roasted duck breasts                                    227
*with braised pearl barley and blackberry sauce*

Spiced braised duck legs                                    228

# Spicy tuna tartare

*with wonton crisps*

This is such an easy-to-prepare starter, yet the stunning results belie the small amount of effort required to make it. It is essential to buy the freshest possible tuna for this dish as it is served raw. Tosa soy is a rich, dark Japanese soy sauce that has been infused with dried tuna flakes. It can be bought online, but if you can't track it down, use a good-quality dark soy sauce instead. Wonton wrappers can also be bought online (try specialist Asian ingredient suppliers) or in some Asian supermarkets.

1. Mix together the soy sauce, chilli-garlic paste and sesame oil in a bowl. Put the tuna into a shallow dish, drizzle over the dressing, then stir to coat the tuna with dressing. Cover and leave in the fridge for 1 hour.

2. Meanwhile, make the wonton crisps. Heat a deep-fat fryer to 180°C or fill a large saucepan one-third full of vegetable oil and heat until a cube of bread dropped in the oil sizzles and turns golden in 30 seconds.

3. Deep-fry the wonton-wrapper halves (in two batches) in the hot oil for about 2 minutes, until golden and crisp. Remove with a slotted spoon and drain on kitchen paper.

4. Divide the tuna mixture among the wonton crisps on four plates. Add a dollop of soured cream and scatter over the spring onions and sesame seeds, then drizzle a little sesame oil on top. Serve immediately.

SERVES 4 AS A STARTER

2 tbsp Tosa soy sauce (or regular dark soy sauce, if you can't get hold of Tosa soy)

50g chilli-garlic paste from a jar *(or see Bang bang chicken salad on page 192 for how to make your own)*

1 tbsp sesame oil, plus extra for drizzling

360g very fresh tuna loin, skinned and diced

Vegetable oil, for deep-frying

8 wonton wrappers, cut in half diagonally to make 16 triangles

2 spring onions, trimmed and shredded

1 tbsp mixed sesame seeds

2 tbsp soured cream

# Stone bass carpaccio

Stone bass is a large, firm-fleshed sea fish that is perfect for carpaccio – slicing very finely and serving raw. If you can't find stone bass in your local fishmonger, this recipe can also be made using sea bass or any firm white fish, but make sure that it is as fresh as possible and that you use it on the day you buy it.

1. Heavily salt the stone bass all over, then place it in a dish and leave for 15–20 minutes in the fridge to remove some of the moisture. Wash off all the salt and pat dry with kitchen paper.

2. Meanwhile, mix the ginger, vinegar, honey and olive oil together in a small bowl, to make a dressing, and season with salt.

3. Halve and stone the avocado, then scoop out the flesh into a food processor. Add the lemon juice, yoghurt and a little salt to season, and blitz together until smooth.

4. Finely slice the stone bass fillet and place on serving plates, then drizzle with the ginger dressing. Spoon some avocado purée on top of each plate of fish, then garnish with the lime zest, and some horseradish, if you like. Serve immediately.

1 very fresh large stone bass fillet, about 200g, skin removed

2.5cm piece of fresh root ginger (about 25g), peeled and finely diced

2 tbsp white wine vinegar

1 tbsp runny honey

5 tbsp extra virgin olive oil

1 ripe avocado

Juice of ½ lemon

1 tbsp natural yoghurt

Sea salt

*To garnish (optional)*

Lime zest

Fresh horseradish root, finely grated

# Pan-fried scallops

*with Jerusalem artichoke purée,*
*apple and crispy chicken skin*

Make sure you choose the best-quality hand-dived scallops for this dish and be careful not to overcook them. We serve them on their shells on a bed of seaweed and topped with crispy chicken skin; both garnishes are optional, but little restaurant flourishes like this can turn a lovely starter into a superb one. It's easy to cook and you can use the chicken breasts for Bang bang chicken salad (see page 192) or Chicken ballotines (see page 224).

1. Make the crispy chicken skin (if using). Preheat the oven to 190°C/170°C fan/Gas 5. Line a baking tray with baking parchment. Remove any excess fat from the underside of the chicken skin. Lay the skin on the lined baking tray, then place another baking tray directly on top. Bake for 20 minutes, until very crispy. Transfer the crispy skin to kitchen paper and leave to drain. Once it's dry and crisp, break the skin into shards and set aside.

2. Melt the butter in a large, wide saucepan, then add the artichokes and a pinch of salt. Cook over a medium heat, stirring occasionally, until they begin to caramelise, 2–3 minutes. Pour over enough milk to cover the slices, then spread them out in an even layer in the pan. Bring to a gentle simmer, then cook, uncovered, over a low–medium heat for 15–20 minutes, until soft. Pour in a little more milk partway through, if necessary, to keep the artichokes covered.

3. Take off the heat, then blitz the artichoke mixture with a stick blender for a few minutes. Add more milk if needed to make a soft purée, then season with salt and pepper to taste. Keep warm.

4. Pour the stock for the dressing into a small saucepan, bring to the boil over a medium heat and reduce to a sticky consistency (to 1½–2 tablespoons), 8–10 minutes. Whisk in the olive oil and lemon juice and set aside. Warm through before serving, if necessary.

5. For the scallops, place a large, non-stick frying pan over a high heat and heat a dash or two of vegetable oil (add more during cooking if needed). Pat the scallops dry with kitchen paper, then season. Cook the scallops, flat side down, for 2–3 minutes or until golden brown underneath. Turn them over and remove the pan from the heat. Leave the scallops in the pan for 1 minute, to cook through, then drain any excess oil on kitchen paper.

6. Place a spoonful of artichoke purée onto each plate, then top with the scallops. Garnish with batons of apple, tarragon leaves and shards of chicken skin (if using). Drizzle over the warm dressing to serve.

*For the crispy chicken skin (optional)*

Skin from 2 chicken breasts (use the flesh for a pie, stir-fry or casserole)

*For the Jerusalem artichoke purée*

15g butter

250g Jerusalem artichokes (or use potatoes, such as King Edward, if you can't get artichokes), washed, scrubbed and finely sliced

About 350–400ml whole milk

Sea salt and freshly ground black pepper

*For the dressing*

150ml good-quality chicken stock

1½ tbsp olive oil

1½ tsp lemon juice

*For the scallops*

About 2 tbsp vegetable oil

8–12 fresh hand-dived or large scallops, depending on size (Orkney ones, if you can get them), cleaned and corals removed

1 dessert apple, such as Braeburn, peeled, cored and cut into small batons

Fresh tarragon leaves, to garnish

# Roast beef carpaccio

*with truffle dressing*

Carpaccio of roast beef makes a really stylish starter, especially if it's garnished with shavings of black truffle – the ultimate foodie luxury. If you want to get ahead, use leftover roast beef, or this dish can be made the day before and kept in the fridge; just take the beef and dressing out of the fridge at least 30 minutes before serving and follow the plating instructions below.

1. Preheat the oven to 200°C/180°C fan/Gas 6. Put the joint of beef into a roasting tray, brush all over with a little oil and season well with salt and pepper, then roast for 15–20 minutes, until it reaches an internal temperature of 36°C. Transfer the joint to a sealable container and set aside to cool. Once cool, cover the container with its lid, then chill in the fridge for at least 2 hours, until cold, or up to 12 hours, before serving.

2. For the dressing, melt the butter in a small frying pan, then add the mushrooms and sauté over a medium heat for 1 minute. Set aside to cool.

3. Once cold, finely chop the mushrooms and place in a bowl. Add the crème fraîche, olive oil, truffle oil and sherry vinegar and whisk together until combined. Season to taste with salt and pepper.

4. Smear the dressing onto four serving plates. Slice the chilled beef as thinly as possible using a very sharp knife, then lay the slices on top of the dressing – depending on how thinly you slice the beef, four or five pieces per serving will be plenty (see Tip). Garnish with frisee, chives, beetroot and cress. Finish with shavings of black truffle, if using, and season with pepper.

SERVES 4 AS A STARTER

600g beef rib eye

Drizzle of vegetable oil

50g frisee lettuce

2 tbsp snipped fresh chives

2 small cooked beetroot, thinly sliced, to serve (optional)

celery cress or mustard cress, to serve

1 medium fresh black truffle (optional)

*For the truffle dressing*

10g butter

20g trompette mushrooms (or use chestnut mushrooms), roughly chopped

100g crème fraîche

2 tbsp olive oil

1 tsp truffle oil

1 tsp sherry vinegar

Sea salt and freshly ground black pepper

TIP
Store any leftover (unsliced) beef in an airtight container in the fridge for up to 3 days, then slice it thinly and use in sandwiches, salads or as part of a cold meat platter.

# Pan-fried cod

*with artichokes and crushed potatoes*

Despite the simple name, this is a stunning, luxurious fish dish that's ideal for a special occasion. Choose thick, meaty cod loin steaks from a sustainable source and baby artichokes when they're in season (late spring and early summer). If you can't get baby artichokes, use two large ones instead. Serve with steamed seasonal green vegetables to offset the rich, buttery potatoes and deliciously crispy fish skin.

1. First prepare the artichokes (see Tip), then drain them. Put the olive oil, lemon juice, white wine and drained artichokes into a saucepan with 50ml water, then add the garlic, bay leaf, thyme and a pinch of salt. Cover tightly with a cartouche (a circle of baking parchment or buttered greaseproof paper – see Tips on page 228), cover the pan with a lid and braise gently for 15–20 minutes, until the artichokes are tender. Remove from the heat and leave the artichokes to cool in the liquid, drain (discarding the cooking liquor, garlic and herbs) and slice.

2. While the artichokes are cooling, cook the potatoes in a pan of salted boiling water for 15–20 minutes or until tender. Meanwhile, melt the butter in a frying pan, add the onion, cover with a lid and cook gently over a low heat, stirring occasionally, for about 20 minutes. After about 15 minutes, the onion will be lovely and soft. Remove the lid and increase the heat slightly, until the onion turns golden and caramelises. This should produce about 2 tablespoons of caramelised onions.

3. Drain the potatoes, then return them to the pan and crush gently with a potato masher. Stir through the capers, olive oil and caramelised onions, then season to taste with salt and pepper. Keep warm while you cook the fish.

4. Heat the olive oil in a frying pan over a high heat until hot. Season the cod, then place the fillets, skin side down, in the pan and cook for 4 minutes. Turn over and cook for a further 2 minutes or longer, depending on the thickness of the fish, until cooked through.

5. Remove the fish to a warm plate and keep hot. Melt the butter in the pan, then cook over a medium heat for 2–3 minutes, until it becomes a deep nut-brown colour, watching it carefully so it doesn't burn. Add the sliced artichokes, lemon segments and chopped herbs, and stir lightly to mix. Stir in the balsamic vinegar to finish.

6. Serve the pan-fried cod fillets and crushed potatoes on warmed plates with the artichoke mixture spooned over. Serve with steamed green beans and peas.

SERVES 4

1 tbsp olive oil
4 cod loin fillets, about 200g each, skin on
40g butter
½ lemon, segmented and chopped
Small handful of fresh flat leaf parsley leaves, chopped
Small handful of fresh tarragon leaves, chopped
2 tsp aged balsamic vinegar

*For the artichokes*
50ml olive oil
Juice of ½ lemon
50ml white wine
4 baby or 2 large artichokes, sliced
1 garlic clove, peeled and left whole
1 bay leaf
2 thyme sprigs
Pinch of sea salt

*For the crushed potatoes*
650g Charlotte potatoes
50g butter
1 large onion, sliced
50g capers, drained weight
50ml olive oil
Sea salt and freshly ground black pepper

TIP
For baby artichokes, remove the outer leaves, then the top third. With a teaspoon scrape out the fluffy fronds in the centre. Peel the stems to remove the green (bitter) part. Place in a bowl of cold water with lemon juice. For large artichokes, peel the thick skin at the base and slice off the stem, then prepare as above.

# Pan-fried hake

*with black pudding and white wine sauce*

This combination of delicate white fish with meaty black pudding, wilted curly kale and tangy white wine sauce is sensational. Hake is a member of the cod family and is similar in texture to cod with a slightly more subtle flavour. It is an excellent sustainable choice, but if you can't find it at your local fishmonger, it can be substituted with cod or haddock.

1. First make the white wine sauce. Melt the butter in a pan, add the shallots, peppercorns and bay leaves, and sauté over a low heat until the shallots have softened and are beginning to colour, 3–4 minutes. Add the white wine, then bubble and reduce over a medium heat until almost completely evaporated, about 5 minutes. Pour in the hot stock and then bubble until reduced by a third, 5–10 minutes. Strain the sauce through a sieve, pushing the pulp through. Return to the pan, stir in the cream and simmer for a few minutes to thicken. Remove from the heat, season with salt and set aside.

2. Heat 2 tablespoons of the olive oil in a pan, add the onion and cook gently for 10–15 minutes, stirring occasionally, until very soft. Add the black pudding and continue to cook for a further 2–3 minutes, until it becomes a little bit crisp. Add the kale, cover and cook for about 5 minutes or until wilted. Season to taste with salt and pepper. Keep warm.

3. Meanwhile, place a frying pan over a medium heat and add the remaining 1 tablespoon of olive oil. Place the hake fillets in the pan, skin side down, and cook for 5 minutes, then turn over and cook for a further 4–5 minutes, depending on the thickness of the fillets, until cooked all the way through. In the meantime, gently reheat the sauce until hot.

4. To serve, spoon the black pudding and kale mixture onto serving plates, place the fish fillets on top, then pour the white wine sauce around the fish and sprinkle with lemon zest.

SERVES 4

3 tbsp olive oil

1 white onion, diced

100g black pudding, diced

300g curly kale, tough stalks removed and leaves chopped

4 hake fillets, about 200g each, skin on

Zest of 1 lemon, to serve

*For the white wine sauce* (see Tip)

25g butter

2 shallots, sliced

5 black peppercorns

2 bay leaves

100ml white wine

400ml hot fish stock

50ml double cream

Sea salt

TIP
The sauce can be made up to a day ahead. Simply make it as directed, then cool, cover and store in the fridge overnight. The next day, reheat it gently until hot, before serving.

# Sea trout

*with clams*

Sea trout, or salmon trout as it's sometimes called, is one of our favourite seasonal treats. It's only available from April to July but is well worth seeking out during this time. A close relation to salmon, the pink flesh tastes similar but is a little more subtle. The clams can be substituted for mussels or cockles if you prefer, but remember to discard any that don't open once cooked.

1. Heat 1 tablespoon of the olive oil in a large saucepan over a high heat until hot. Add the shellfish and toss a couple of times. Add the white wine, put the lid on the pan and cook for 2 minutes, until the shellfish have opened. Check them and discard any that are still closed, then pour the shellfish and juice into a heatproof bowl and set aside.

2. Pour the hot fish stock into the same pan, along with all the vegetables and cook over a medium heat for about 4 minutes, until the vegetables are al dente.

3. Lift out the vegetables using a slotted spoon and place in a separate pan. Strain the shellfish juice into the stock pan. Add the shellfish to the vegetables with the parsley and cover with a lid to keep warm. Gradually whisk the 50ml oil into the hot stock to emulsify into a sauce. Season with salt and pepper. Keep warm.

4. Cook the sea trout. Heat the remaining 1 tablespoon of olive oil in a large frying pan over a medium heat until hot. Add the trout fillets to the pan (cook them in a couple of batches, if necessary), skin side down, and cook over a low–medium heat for 3 minutes (per batch). Remove the cooked fillets to a plate.

5. Once all the trout fillets are cooked and on one side, add the garlic, thyme and butter to the pan and heat until the butter is melted. Return the fillets to the pan (again, you may need to do this in batches) and cook on the other side for a further 2 minutes, all the while glazing them with the melted butter. Add the garlic, thyme and butter to the pan. Turn the fish over and cook for a further 2 minutes, all the while glazing it with the melted butter. The fish should be served pink in the middle.

6. Put a large ladleful of vegetables, shellfish and a little of the emulsified stock/sauce into each serving bowl, then place the trout fillets on top and drizzle over any pan juices, if you like. Garnish with the lemon zest and serve with fresh bread to mop up the delicious juices.

SERVES 6

50ml olive oil, plus 2 tbsp

500g clams, mussels or cockles in shell, cleaned (see Tip)

50ml white wine

500ml good-quality hot fish stock

½ Romanesco broccoli, divided into florets (or use standard broccoli or cauliflower)

6 baby carrots, peeled and finely sliced lengthways

½ fennel bulb, trimmed and finely sliced

6 asparagus spears, finely sliced

6 stems rainbow chard, sliced

1 small yellow and green courgette, diced

2 tbsp chopped parsley

6 sea trout fillets, about 160–180g each, skin on (or use salmon)

3 garlic cloves, crushed

6 thyme sprigs

50–75g butter

Sea salt and freshly ground black pepper

Finely grated zest of 1 lemon, to garnish

TIPS

To clean shellfish, place in a bowl and cover with cold water, drain then pull away beards. Scrub mussels with a stiff nail brush. Tap open shellfish sharply with the back of a knife – if they don't close, discard them.

You can make this dish later in the summer with slightly bigger turnips and swapping asparagus for broad and runner beans.

# Chicken ballotines

*with potato wedges and spicy broccoli*

Chicken wrapped in bacon is an oldie but a goodie and when you add fresh sage and cook it in white wine, you elevate this favourite to a special dish, perfect for serving to friends and family. The garlic and chilli-flavoured broccoli and paprika-spiced potato wedges are cracking side dishes worth keeping up your sleeve for serving with duck, lamb, steak or fish dishes.

1. Preheat the oven to 220°C/200°C fan/Gas 7.

2. Place the potato wedges in a roasting tray, sprinkle with the paprika and 2 teaspoons of the oil, season with salt and toss to coat. Roast for 20–30 minutes, until cooked, golden and crispy.

3. Meanwhile, blanch the broccoli in a pan of salted boiling water for 3–4 minutes, until just tender. Drain, immediately plunge into a bowl of iced water until cool, then drain again and set aside.

4. For the ballotines, place the halved bacon rashers alongside each other on a chopping board, then put a slice of chicken on top of each. Season with salt and pepper. Roll up each rasher to enclose the chicken, securing with a cocktail stick.

5. Heat 1 tablespoon of the remaining oil in a large frying pan over a medium heat until hot – use a pan that can hold all the chicken rolls, or cook them in a batches. Place the chicken rolls in the pan in a single layer and cook for 3–4 minutes, until caramelised underneath. Turn over and cook for a further 2–3 minutes, until golden. Set aside.

6. Pour the wine into the pan and bubble over a medium heat, until reduced by half, 1–2 minutes. Return the chicken to the pan in an even layer – they might be quite snug. Cover with a lid and cook for 4–5 minutes, until all the rolls are cooked through. To check, slice one roll in half through the thickest part – there should be no pink juices.

7. Meanwhile, heat the remaining 2 teaspoons of oil in a separate large frying pan, until hot. Add the garlic and chilli, and cook for a couple of minutes without colouring. Add the blanched broccoli and toss it in the oil until warmed through, about 3 minutes.

8. Transfer the cooked chicken rolls to a plate and keep warm. Add the hot stock, butter and chopped sage to the pan and scrape up all the tasty bits from the bottom, then bubble over a medium heat for a couple of minutes, until the sauce thickens.

9. Remove the cocktail sticks from the chicken and divide among serving plates. Pour over the sauce and serve with the broccoli and potato wedges.

SERVES 4-6

750g roasting potatoes (such as King Edward or Desirée), washed and cut into wedges

1 tsp paprika

35ml extra virgin olive oil

250–375g Tenderstem broccoli, trimmed

16 rashers of smoked streaky bacon, cut in half widthways

4 chicken breast fillets (preferably corn-fed), each sliced widthways into 4 thin slices

50ml white wine

1 garlic clove, chopped

1 red chilli, deseeded and chopped

100ml hot chicken stock

50g butter

Small bunch of fresh sage chopped

Sea salt and freshly ground black pepper

# Pan-roasted duck breasts

*with braised pearl barley and blackberry sauce*

The richness of duck is brilliantly offset by fruity sauces, such as with this fresh blackberry one. The sharpness of the berries cuts through the fattiness of the duck and balances the dish perfectly. Duck breasts should be served pink in the middle to ensure the dense meat stays tender, so don't be tempted to cook it for much longer than the time stipulated.

1. For the braised pearl barley, heat the oil in a saucepan, add the leek, carrots, celery and garlic, and cook gently, stirring occasionally, until softened, about 10 minutes. Add the pearl barley and cook for 2 minutes, stirring constantly. Pour in the wine and bubble over a medium heat for a few minutes, stirring often, until it has almost all been absorbed, then stir in the hot stock and herb sprigs.

2. Cover tightly with a cartouche (a circle of baking parchment or buttered greaseproof paper – see Tip on page 228) and cook over a low–medium heat for 20–25 minutes, until the barley is al dente. Keep warm and discard the herb stalks before serving.

3. Meanwhile, for the blackberry sauce, put the blackberries, sugar and port into a saucepan, cover with a lid and cook gently for 5–10 minutes, until the blackberries are soft but still holding their shape (you don't want them to become too soft and lose their shape).

4. Pour the beef jus into a separate saucepan and heat gently until hot, then remove from the heat. Using a slotted spoon, transfer the softened blackberries to the beef jus pan along with 50ml of the blackberry cooking liquor (discard the rest) and stir gently to combine. Keep warm while you cook the duck.

5. Preheat the oven to 240°C/220°C fan/Gas 9.

6. Lightly score the fat on each duck breast using a sharp knife, then season each one with salt. Put the duck breasts, fat side down, into a cold, heavy-based ovenproof frying pan. Cook over a low–medium heat for 8–10 minutes, allowing the fat to render.

7. Turn the duck breasts over so that the fat is facing up, then transfer the pan to the oven and cook for 4–5 minutes, until the skin is crispy and the meat is browned on the outside but pink in the middle. Remove from the oven and let the duck rest for 5 minutes before carving.

8. Spoon the braised pearl barley onto serving plates, place the duck breasts on top, then pour over the blackberry sauce.

SERVES 4

4 duck breasts, skin on

Sea salt

*For the braised pearl barley*

3 tbsp vegetable oil

1 leek, chopped

2 carrots, peeled and diced

2 celery sticks, trimmed and diced

3 garlic cloves, crushed

250g pearl barley

200ml white wine

1 litre hot vegetable or chicken stock

3 thyme sprigs

3 rosemary sprigs

*For the blackberry sauce*

100g fresh blackberries

20g caster sugar

100ml port

300ml Beef jus (see page 234)

# Spiced braised duck legs

Most of the work for this braised duck dish is done up front (leaving you plenty of time to get ready for your guests), plus it has the added bonus that your kitchen will smell amazing by the time everyone arrives. The duck legs are braised slowly in a low oven until the meat is very tender, then the braising stock is strained and reduced to produce a lovely syrupy sauce to spoon over the duck to serve.

1. Preheat the oven to 170°C/150°C fan/Gas 3.

2. Heat a large frying pan until hot, then reduce the heat to medium, add the duck legs, in batches, and cook for about 8 minutes, until the skin is crisp and golden brown. Take care that the fat released from the duck doesn't spit too much; if it does, reduce the heat slightly. Remove the duck legs to a plate and set aside.

3. Heat the oil in a large, wide casserole, add all the vegetables, the garlic, bay leaf, thyme and rosemary, and cook over a medium heat for 10 minutes, stirring occasionally, until caramelised. Stir in the tomato purée and cook for a further 2 minutes.

4. Add all the spices, then pour in the apple juice and stock. Stir everything together and then place the duck legs back in the casserole, making sure they are covered with the liquid. Cover tightly with a cartouche (a circle of baking parchment or buttered greaseproof paper – see Tip) and braise in the oven for 2 hours, until very tender.

5. Remove from the oven, then lift the duck legs out of the sauce and set aside on a large plate. Cover and keep warm in the turned-off (or very low) oven.

6. Strain the liquid into a bowl (reserve the vegetables – see Tip). Lift off and discard as much fat as possible, then return the stock to the casserole and place over a high heat. Bring to the boil, then reduce the heat to medium and simmer for 30 minutes, until the stock has reduced to a syrupy sauce.

7. Put a duck leg onto each plate, spoon over the sauce and serve with Beetroot and Cranberry Chutney (see page 232) and steamed hispi cabbage.

SERVES 8

8 duck legs, skin on
1 tbsp vegetable oil
2 carrots, peeled and roughly chopped
1 onion, roughly chopped
2 celery sticks, trimmed and roughly chopped
1 leek, trimmed and roughly chopped
4 garlic cloves, left whole and unpeeled
1 bay leaf
4 thyme sprigs
2 rosemary sprigs
1½ tbsp tomato purée
1 green cardamom pod, left whole
1 star anise
3 black peppercorns
½ cinnamon stick
800ml apple juice
1.5 litres chicken stock
Sea salt

TIPS
To make a cartouche, cut out a circle of baking parchment, the same size as the top of the casserole or pan, then fold it in half and half and half again, and so on, until it becomes a very thin triangle. Open this out again and place it in the casserole/pan. The creases help to create a tighter fit when it's placed on the surface of the food.

Save the strained vegetables (discard the herbs and spices) – they're delicious spread on toasted sourdough and served with some crumbled feta cheese sprinkled over the top.

# Venison ragu

Venison is a lean but rich meat that falls apart when you cook it using this low and slow method. The resulting ragu is meltingly soft but big on flavour and the perfect dish for a laid-back kitchen supper with friends. It can also be made a day or so in advance, then reheated – in fact, it will be better for it as the flavours really develop over time.

1. Pour the beef stock into a saucepan and bring to the boil, then bubble over a medium heat until reduced by half, about 15 minutes (you need 1 litre of beef stock). Set aside.

2. Meanwhile, heat the vegetable oil in a large, heavy-based casserole, then add the diced venison (in a couple or so batches) and cook until nicely coloured all over, about 5 minutes. Remove each batch of browned meat to a plate, while you continue to brown the rest (adding a little extra oil if needed), then remove the last batch from the casserole.

3. Add all the diced vegetables to the casserole (adding a little extra oil if needed) and cook over a medium heat for about 10 minutes, stirring occasionally, until nicely caramelised. Stir in the tomato purée and cook for a few minutes. Pour in the red wine and Madeira to deglaze the casserole, scraping up any bits from the bottom and bubbling the liquids until reduced by half.

4. Return the browned meat to the casserole and add the reduced beef stock, the juniper berries and rosemary. Cover and cook over a low–medium heat for 1½–2 hours, stirring occasionally, until the venison is very tender and the sauce has thickened, removing the lid about halfway through cooking. When the meat is ready, you should be able to break a piece in half easily with two forks.

5. When the ragu is nearly ready, cook the pappardelle in a large pan of boiling salted water until al dente, according to the packet instructions.

6. Meanwhile, for the garnish, if using, melt the butter in a frying pan, add the garlic and sauté for a minute without colouring. Stir in the breadcrumbs and cook over a low heat for about 10 minutes, until golden and toasted, stirring regularly to make sure they don't burn. Stir in the parsley.

7. Drain the cooked pasta. Season the ragu with the Worcestershire sauce and discard the rosemary stalks. Serve the ragu with the cooked pappardelle and sprinkle with the toasted breadcrumb garnish, if using, and grated Parmesan.

SERVES 4-6

2 litres beef stock

1 tbsp vegetable oil, plus extra as needed

1kg diced venison

¼ celeriac (about 150g), peeled and diced

¼ butternut squash (about 200g), peeled, deseeded and diced

¼ swede (about 150g), peeled and diced

1 onion, diced

3 tbsp tomato purée

750ml red wine

100ml Madeira

1 tbsp (about 5g) juniper berries

10g rosemary sprigs

800g fresh pappardelle

5 tbsp Worcestershire sauce

50g Parmesan cheese, grated, for sprinkling

*For the garnish (optional)*

25g butter

2 garlic cloves, crushed

150g fresh white breadcrumbs

1 tbsp finely chopped fresh flat leaf parsley

# Beetroot and cranberry chutney

We serve this sweet and sour chutney with the Spiced braised duck legs (see page 228), but it also makes a great accompaniment to cold ham or beef, smoked fish or cheese. It is ready to eat as soon as it's cooked and cooled, but it will also keep well in sterilised jars for a week or so before opening. A pretty jar of bright purple chutney makes a lovely present too.

1. Preheat the oven to 200°C/180°C fan/Gas 6. Wrap the beetroot together in foil, place the package on a baking sheet and bake until tender, about 1¼–1¾ hours (depending on size), turning each beetroot over halfway through (then re-wrapping).

2. Once cooked, remove from the oven, unwrap and leave until cool enough to handle. Cut each beetroot in half widthways, peel, then grate on the coarse side of the grater.

3. Heat the vegetable oil in a large saucepan, add the onions and cook over a low heat, stirring occasionally, until soft but not coloured, about 20–25 minutes. Add the grated beetroot, 250g of the (still frozen) cranberries (leave the remaining 50g to thaw out for adding later), the sugar, port and both vinegars and simmer slowly, uncovered, over a low heat for about 30 minutes, stirring every now and then, until most of the liquid has been absorbed into the mixture so it blends together, but the mix is still juicy and the cranberries are well softened.

4. Once the beetroot mixture is ready, stir in the reserved thawed cranberries (to provide extra texture) and cook for 4–5 minutes.

5. Spoon the chutney into hot, sterilised jars (see Tip on page 80). To squash out any air bubbles, jiggle a teaspoon up and down in the jar. Seal with vinegar-proof lids and leave until cold. Serve once cold, or store in a cool, dark place for up to a week before opening so the flavours can mellow a bit more. Once opened, store in the fridge for up to a month.

MAKES ABOUT 1 LITRE
(ENOUGH TO FILL ABOUT
4 X 350G JARS)

8 raw red beetroot (about 875g in total), ends trimmed (see Tip), rinsed and patted dry

2 tbsp vegetable oil

2 red onions (about 325g in total), halved and very thinly sliced

300g frozen cranberries

115g light soft brown sugar

125ml ruby port

3 tbsp balsamic vinegar

2 tbsp red wine vinegar

TIP
When preparing the beetroot, don't trim the root and leaf ends too near to the beetroot flesh, or it will bleed during cooking. Also, if you leave a bit of each end on, it gives you something to hold on to when grating the beetroot later.

# Beef jus

Often the biggest difference between cooking at home and eating out is the quality and depth of the sauces. In restaurant kitchens, the stocks are made from scratch, then intensified with aromatics and wine before being reduced and seasoned well, resulting in rich and velvety sauces, like these beef and chicken jus (opposite). There is no reason why this process can't be done at home, injecting some of that restaurant magic into your own cooking.

1. Season the beef trimmings well with salt and pepper. Heat the oil in a large pan until smoking hot, then add the beef (you may need to do this in a couple of batches; if so, use 1 tablespoon of oil per batch) and cook over a medium heat, until well coloured all over, about 5 minutes per batch. Remove the beef trimmings to a plate and set aside.

2. Add the shallots, garlic and bouquet garni to the pan, then cook over a low-medium heat, until the shallots are softened, about 5 minutes.

3. Return the beef trimmings to the pan, pour in the port to deglaze the pan, scraping up the bits from the bottom, then cook over a medium heat until reduced by half, about 10 minutes. Do the same with the red wine, reducing it by half, about 15 minutes. Stir in the stock and bring to the boil, then bubble, uncovered, over a medium heat for about 2 hours, until reduced and a rich, dark brown colour.

4. Strain the mixture through a fine sieve into a clean pan. Add the thyme sprigs, bring to the boil, then bubble over a medium heat until reduced to about 300ml, about 8 minutes. It should be a nice coating consistency over the back of a spoon – thinner than a gravy, but thicker than a stock.

5. Adjust the seasoning to taste, strain into a warm jug and serve (see Tip).

MAKES ABOUT 300ML

500g beef trimmings

2 tbsp vegetable oil

2 shallots, chopped

2 garlic cloves, unpeeled and lightly smashed with the flat of a large knife

1 fresh bouquet garni (1 thyme sprig, 1 parsley sprig and 1 bay leaf)

190ml port

1.5 litres red wine

1.5 litres veal or beef stock

2 thyme sprigs

Sea salt and freshly ground black pepper

TIP
Once made, the beef jus can be cooled, then stored in an airtight container in the fridge for up to 5 days (or you can freeze it for up to a month). Reheat gently (thawing it first, if frozen) before serving.

# Chicken jus

1. Preheat the oven to 200°C/180°C fan/Gas 6.

2. Place the chicken wings in a single layer in a large, hob-proof roasting tray. Roast for 1 hour, until golden brown all over.

3. Heat the oil in a large stockpot or saucepan until hot, add the shallots, garlic and bouquet garni, and cook over a medium heat, until softened, about 5 minutes.

4. Remove the chicken wings from the oven and carefully pour off and discard the excess fat. Transfer the chicken wings to the stockpot. Set the roasting tray over a medium heat on the hob. Pour in the wine to deglaze the tray, scraping up the bits from the bottom, then cook over a medium heat until reduced by half, about 5–8 minutes.

5. Pour the reduced wine into the stockpot, then pour in the chicken stock and 500ml water to cover the chicken wings. Season with salt and pepper and bring to the boil, then bubble over a low heat, with the pan half-covered with a lid, for 1 hour.

6. Strain the mixture through a fine sieve into a clean pan (see Tip). Bring to the boil, then bubble over a medium–high heat, until reduced to about 300ml, about 25 minutes. It should be a nice coating consistency over the back of a spoon – thinner than a gravy, but thicker than a stock.

7. Stir in a dash of sherry vinegar, adjust the seasoning to taste, then pour into a warm jug and serve (see Tip).

MAKES ABOUT 300ML

500g chicken wings

1 tbsp vegetable oil

4 shallots, chopped

2 garlic cloves, unpeeled and lightly smashed with the flat of a large knife

1 fresh bouquet garni (1 thyme sprig, 1 parsley sprig and 1 bay leaf)

200ml white wine

1 litre fresh chicken stock

Dash of sherry vinegar

Sea salt and freshly ground black pepper

TIPS

Once the chicken wings are cooked and strained, pull off any cooked meat and keep it to add to a fresh tomato pasta sauce or stir through cooked rice. If you are not using the meat straightaway, then cool it and store in the fridge.

Once made, the chicken jus can be cooled, then stored in an airtight container in the fridge for up to 5 days (or you can freeze it for up to a month). Reheat gently (thawing it first, if frozen) before serving.

# Honey panna cotta

This lovely panna cotta has to be left to set overnight, so it's a great dessert for entertaining – no last-minute baking or flambéing here. The dill- and elderflower-infused cucumber may seem a bit out of place, but the combination of these flavours with the creamy panna cotta is exquisite.

MAKES 4

2½ sheets of leaf gelatine

500ml double or whipping cream

3 tbsp whole milk

70g runny honey

Flavourless oil, for greasing

½ cucumber, peeled and diced

1 tbsp chopped fresh dill

75ml elderflower cordial

25g caster sugar

2 ripe apricots, quartered

Icing sugar, for dusting

Fresh chopped dill, to decorate

1. Place the gelatine leaves in a small bowl of cold water and leave for 3–5 minutes, until softened.

2. Put the cream, milk and honey into a saucepan, and heat gently until almost boiling (about 90°C), then remove from the heat. Squeeze out the gelatine and add to the cream mixture, stirring well until the gelatine is completely dissolved. Set aside to cool slightly.

3. Meanwhile, have ready 4 x 150ml panna cotta or dariole moulds. If they are plastic, rinse in cold water, but don't dry them; if they are metal, grease them lightly with a flavourless vegetable oil. This will make the panna cottas easier to turn out once set.

4. Pour the panna cotta mixture through a sieve into a jug, then pour into the waiting moulds. Place in the fridge and leave to set overnight.

5. Meanwhile, mix together the cucumber and dill in a bowl, then cover and leave to infuse in the fridge overnight.

6. The next day, put the elderflower cordial, sugar and 50ml water into a small pan and cook gently, stirring until the sugar has dissolved, then bring to the boil. Remove from the heat and leave to cool completely, before pouring over the cucumber–dill mix.

7. When ready to serve, place a frying pan over a high heat. When the pan is hot, dip the apricot quarters in icing sugar and cook for 30 seconds on each side.

8. To serve, dip the moulds briefly (about 5 seconds) in boiling water. Place a serving plate over each one and, holding tightly, invert both, giving the mould a little shake if necessary to release each panna cotta. Serve the panna cottas with the infused cucumber (with a little of the syrup), together with the caramelised apricots, and decorate with chopped dill.

# Pineapple carpaccio

## *with coconut sorbet*

This BSK classic is a brilliantly refreshing dish to serve at the end of an indulgent meal. The tropical flavours of the pineapple and passion fruit are given an even more exotic boost by the star anise, plus a welcome zestiness from the lime. If you don't want to make the coconut sorbet, the pineapple carpaccio is just as delicious served with a scoop of good-quality vanilla ice cream.

1. Make the sorbet in advance (up to a week ahead). Pierce holes in the coconut and drain the water from inside (you can reserve this and use it in a smoothie). Crack the shell and remove the coconut flesh. Peel away and discard the brown skin, using either a sharp knife or a vegetable peeler, then blend the flesh pieces in a food processor until finely chopped.

2. Put the milk, coconut milk and sugar into a saucepan, and heat gently, stirring, until the sugar has dissolved, then bring to the boil. Stir in the finely chopped coconut and bring back to the boil. Remove from the heat, then stir in the Malibu. Leave to cool, then churn in an ice-cream machine until frozen (see Tip).

3. Once the sorbet is ready, spoon it into a freezerproof airtight container and store in the freezer until needed. Transfer it to the fridge about 20 minutes or so before serving to soften slightly, if necessary. If you are making and serving the sorbet on the day, it can be served straight from the ice-cream machine, if you like (it will be a softer texture).

4. To make the pineapple carpaccio, put the sugar into a small saucepan with 100ml of water, the lemon juice and star anise, and heat gently, stirring until the sugar has dissolved and the mixture is warm. Remove from the heat.

5. Peel the pineapple, then slice thinly into 8–12 rounds using a very sharp knife. Place in a shallow dish or bowl, pour over the warm syrup and set aside at room temperature for 2 hours.

6. To serve, drain the pineapple slices and divide them among 4 plates (adding a little of the syrup, too, if you like; otherwise discard it). Cut each passion fruit in half and scoop out the flesh, then spoon it on top of the pineapple, allowing the flesh from one passion fruit per plate. Scatter with kiwi. Finish each with a scoop of coconut sorbet (keep any leftover in the freezer for another time) and a sprinkle of lime zest. Serve immediately.

SERVES 4 (*sorbet serves 8*)

*For the coconut sorbet*
1 fresh coconut
150ml whole milk
125ml coconut milk
250g caster sugar
1 tbsp Malibu or other coconut-flavoured rum

*For the pineapple carpaccio*
100g caster sugar
Juice of 1 lemon
3 star anise
½ medium pineapple
4 passion fruit
Finely grated zest of 1 lime
1 kiwi, peeled and diced

TIP
If you are making the sorbet by hand, leave the coconut mixture to cool, then pour into a shallow freezerproof container and chill in the fridge for 30 minutes. Transfer to the freezer and freeze until the sorbet is almost frozen, then whisk well and return to the freezer. Repeat the whisking process every 30 minutes or so, returning it to the freezer each time, until the sorbet is solid.

# Chocolate fondants

The perfect chocolate fondant holds its shape when you turn it out onto the plate but releases a stream of molten chocolate as you cut into it with a spoon. The trick to getting it right (and impressing your friends) is all in the timing, so once 15 minutes of the cooking time has passed, check the fondants by shaking them gently – they are ready when only the centre moves a little. If this isn't the case, return them to the oven and keep checking until it is.

1. Preheat the oven to 190°C/170°C fan/Gas 5. Grease 4 x 220ml dariole moulds or ramekins with butter, place them on a baking sheet and set aside.

2. Put the butter and chocolate into a large heatproof bowl set over a pan of gently simmering water (don't let the bottom of the bowl touch the water underneath) and leave until melted, stirring occasionally. Remove from the heat, sift over the flour and then whisk it in.

3. In a separate bowl, whisk together the eggs, egg yolks and sugar until combined, then whisk this into the chocolate mixture, until smooth and well combined. Pour the chocolate mixture into the prepared dariole moulds or ramekins, dividing evenly. Bake for 15–20 minutes – the fondants are ready when you shake each one gently and only the middle moves a little.

4. Remove from the oven, and then, using a sharp knife, gently loosen around the inside edge of each mould, if necessary. Carefully invert each fondant onto a serving plate and serve immediately with crème fraîche, whipped cream or vanilla ice cream.

SERVES 4 (*easily doubled*)

150g butter, plus extra for greasing

150g dark chocolate (60–70% cocoa solids), roughly chopped or broken into small chunks

75g plain flour

3 large eggs

3 large egg yolks

200g caster sugar

Vanilla ice cream, crème fraîche or whipped cream, to serve

# Cox's Orange Pippin tarte Tatin

Cox's apples are considered by many to be the finest of the English varieties of dessert apple and, as such, they make an excellent choice for a tarte Tatin. As well as being naturally sweet, the flesh has a light acidity that works really well with the wonderful caramel sauce and rich, buttery pastry. If you can't get hold of Cox's, use your favourite dessert apples instead, but choose ones that are not overly sweet.

1. Put the apple quarters in a single layer on kitchen paper on a baking tray, then place them, uncovered, in the fridge and leave to dry out overnight. The apples will go brown, which is correct. This draws out the moisture and concentrates the flavour.

2. The next day, preheat the oven to 200°C/180°C fan/Gas 6.

3. Put the sugar into a large saucepan with 50ml of water. Heat gently, stirring until the sugar has completely dissolved, then increase the heat to medium and continue to cook, without stirring, until the mixture caramelises and becomes a rich, dark colour, 12–15 minutes.

4. Remove the pan from the heat and let the bubbles subside. Carefully place the apple quarters in the hot pan, give them a quick stir with a wooden spoon, then return to the heat. Cook over a medium heat for 2–3 minutes.

5. Add the butter to the pan, stir to mix with the caramel and cook for a further 4–5 minutes. The apples will now be almost cooked but should still hold their shape. If not, cook for another minute or two. Remove from the heat and cool for a minute or so.

6. Take a large 23cm ovenproof frying pan or a tarte Tatin tin, measuring 23cm diameter x 4.5cm deep (see Tip) and arrange the caramelised apples in the pan or tin in circles, cut sides down.

7. Roll out the puff pastry on a lightly floured surface to 5mm thick and, using a plate slightly larger than the top of the pan, cut out a large circle. Place the pastry circle over the apples and tuck it in around the inside edges of the pan. Pierce the pastry a few times with the tip of a sharp knife. Pour the caramel left in the saucepan into a measuring jug, then drizzle some of it around the edge of the pastry into the apples until it is visible just below the level of the pastry. Reserve the remaining caramel sauce for later. Transfer the pan to the oven and bake for about 20 minutes, until the pastry is risen, crisp and golden.

8. Remove from the oven, leave to stand in the pan for about 5 minutes, then loosen the sides and carefully invert the tart onto a serving plate with a rim (to catch the juices), so the apples are facing up. Drizzle with any leftover caramel, cut into wedges and serve with vanilla or cinnamon ice cream.

SERVES 4

5 Cox's Orange Pippin dessert apples, peeled, quartered and cored

200g caster sugar

50g butter

350–400g ready-made all-butter puff pastry

Plain flour, for dusting

Vanilla or cinnamon ice cream, to serve

TIP

You can make four individual tartes Tatin, if you prefer. Use four individual 12cm ovenproof frying pans and arrange the caramelised apples in the pans, dividing evenly. Using 500g puff pastry, cut out four smaller pastry circles to fit the pans, then place over the apples and continue as above. Bake the individual tarts for 15–20 minutes.

# Chocolate tart

The dark chocolate filling for these individual tarts is silky smooth, rich and incredibly indulgent. As there are very few ingredients for the filling, always use a good-quality dark chocolate with at least 70% cocoa solids; the flavour of the finished tarts depends on it.

1. Make the pastry. Cream the butter and sugar together in a bowl until light, then beat in one of the beaten eggs. Gradually stir in the flour and salt, adding a third of the flour at a time, bringing it together to a very soft dough. Briefly work into a ball with your hands, but do not overhandle. Pat flat, wrap in cling film and chill in the fridge for about 1 hour. If the dough still feels soft, chill it a bit longer.

2. Roll out the pastry on a lightly floured surface to about 3mm thick, then cut out 8 x 13cm rounds and use to line eight 9.5cm diameter x 2cm deep, fluted loose-based tart tins, leaving some excess pastry overhanging the rims. Reserve any leftover pastry for patching. Prick the bases all over, then chill for 30 minutes.

3. Preheat the oven to 200°C/180°C fan/Gas 6. Place the pastry-lined tins on a large baking sheet. Line the pastry cases with baking parchment and fill with ceramic baking beans or uncooked rice. Bake 'blind' for 10–12 minutes. Remove from the oven, remove the baking beans and paper, then patch up any cracks with the reserved raw pastry. Brush the remaining egg over the pastry. Return to the oven for 5 minutes, until cooked and pale golden.

4. Remove from the oven and reduce the oven temperature to 120°C/Gas ½ (don't use the fan oven setting). While still warm, use a sharp knife to trim off the excess pastry level with the rim of the tins, then brush out any loose crumbs from inside the cases. Leave to cool completely in the tins.

5. Make the filling. Put the chocolate into a large heatproof bowl. Pour the milk and cream into a small saucepan and bring gently to the boil, then immediately pour over the chocolate. Let it sit for a few minutes to melt the chocolate, then very gently (you don't want to create air bubbles) stir until smooth. Gently fold in the beaten eggs, then combine with a stick blender for a minute or two, until smooth and glossy – keep the blades immersed to prevent creating air bubbles.

6. Carefully pour the chocolate mixture into the pastry cases, dividing it evenly. Use a chef's blow torch (if you have one) to remove any surface bubbles (or use a cocktail stick). Carefully transfer the baking sheet to the oven and bake for 30–35 minutes, until the filling is just set and smooth on the surface.

7. Leave the tarts to cool and set completely before removing from the tins. Serve with pouring cream, honeycomb pieces and/or raspberry sorbet, if you like.

MAKES 8

*For the pastry*
125g butter, softened
75g icing sugar, sifted
2 large eggs, beaten separately
250g plain flour, plus extra for dusting
Pinch of sea salt

*For the filling*
300g dark chocolate (about 70% cocoa solids), very finely chopped
100ml whole milk
200ml double cream
2 large eggs, beaten

*To serve (optional)*
Pouring cream
Honeycomb pieces or crushed honeycomb
Raspberry sorbet

TIPS
To cut the bitterness of the chocolate in the filling, add 1–2 tablespoons of caster sugar to the milk and cream, if you like.

You can make one large tart if you prefer, using a 24cm pastry case (see Cherry Bakewell Tart recipe on page 164). Put the blind-baked tart case (in its tin) on a baking sheet, then pour in the chocolate mixture to fill the case and remove any surface bubbles as in step 6. Bake at 120°C/Gas ½ for about 50 minutes. Leave the tart to cool and set completely before removing it from the tin.

# Blueberry and basil vodka sour

This recipe calls for the blueberries and basil leaves to be 'muddled' together in the bottom of a cocktail shaker, but we don't mean to spin them round and confuse them! A muddler is a bar tool, a bit like a pestle, used for pounding solid ingredients before shaking them with liquids. If you don't have one, use a pestle to muddle the summery flavours in this stunning drink.

1. Muddle the blueberries and basil leaves very well in the bottom of a cocktail shaker.

2. Pour in the vodka, lime juice and sugar syrup, and add a small handful of ice cubes. Shake the cocktail shaker very firmly until the drink is very cold.

3. Place a couple of ice cubes in a tall glass, then strain the liquid into the glass over the ice.

4. Put the remaining blueberries and basil leaf on top of the glass to garnish, then serve.

SERVES 1

4 blueberries, plus 2 for the garnish

2 fresh basil leaves, plus 1 for the garnish

50ml vodka

1 tbsp lime juice

1 tsp caster sugar, dissolved in 1 tsp hot water to create a syrup

Ice cubes

# Savage Garden

Champagne cocktails are perfect for opening the evening with a touch of sparkle and are sure to get everyone in the mood. These two versions show how versatile this aperitif can be: the Savage Garden is made fruity and aromatic with the addition of fig liqueur, while lychees and lavender make Mood Indigo exotic and floral.

1. Pour all the ingredients, except the Champagne, into a cocktail shaker over ice and shake vigorously.

2. Strain into a flute glass and top up with Champagne.

SERVES 1

30ml fig liqueur

15ml gin

10ml fresh lemon juice

Ice cubes

Champagne, to serve

# Mood Indigo

1. Pour all the ingredients, except the Champagne, into a cocktail shaker over ice and shake vigorously.

2. Strain into a flute glass and top up with Champagne.

SERVES 1

20ml gin

15ml lychee purée

10ml fresh lemon juice

10ml lavender syrup

Ice cubes

Champagne, to serve

# Hot toddy

There is nothing more warming and restorative than a hot toddy on a cold winter's night. Made with a combination of Calvados, lemon, honey, orange and spices, then topped up with boiling water, it's definitely medicinal rather than indulgent! Calvados is an apple brandy from Normandy in France and it makes a delightful substitute for whisky.

1. Put all the ingredients, except the boiling water, into a thick, heatproof glass.

2. Top up with boiling water, infuse briefly, stir and serve.

SERVES 1

50ml Calvados

1 tbsp fresh lemon juice

2 tsp runny honey

1 cinnamon stick

1 strip of orange peel, with 4 cloves attached

Slice of fresh root ginger

Boiling water, to serve

# Particularly indulgent hot chocolate

Rewarding yourself at the end of a long day with a hot milky drink is sure to help you sleep. It might sound odd to put a teaspoon of butter into your hot chocolate, but we urge you to try it. It makes it even more velvety and luxurious and adds a tiny bit of salt that enhances the flavour of the chocolate.

1. Put the milk, cream, butter and sugar syrup into a small saucepan, and cook gently for a few minutes, stirring, until almost boiling.

2. Put the cocoa powder into a mug and pour in the hot milk mixture. Stir well until thoroughly mixed, then serve.

SERVES 1

100ml whole milk

1 tbsp double cream

1 tsp butter

1 tbsp simple sugar syrup (see Vodka sour, page 247)

2 tsp cocoa powder (preferably 80%)

# Index

# Acknowledgements

This book is dedicated to the amazing team at Bread Street Kitchen in London and at all our locations around the world. Every waiter, kitchen porter, sommelier, barman, chef and every back-of-house team member have all made a contribution to making all of the Bread Streets such a huge success. So thank you all.

For the great BSK food and the recipes in this book, thanks go to executive head chef, Erion Karaj and his team: Paul Shearing, Guy Betteridge, Sabrina Stillheart, Philip Cardy, Dario Catapano, Michael Turner, Luke Ferguson, Matteo Maritati and Naoufel Gribi. Thanks to general manager Mat Horvath and his front-of-house team for allowing us to take over the restaurant for the photoshoots and to bar manager Paul Hogg and Sotirios Sakkas for the drinks. Cheers guys!

The editorial team that put this book together in record time deserves a big round of applause. Thanks to Camilla Stoddart, our in-house writer, who made things happen at the Bread Street end; to copy-editor, Anne Sheasby, who did an incredible job of whipping the recipes into shape with the help of indefatigable testers Emma Marsden, Sam Dixon and Angela Nilsen; and to Helena Caldon for so calmly picking up the baton and putting the book to bed.

Thank you to the good people at Hodder for their unflappable confidence in this project and their customary professionalism. Thanks to Nicky Ross and Sarah Hammond for steering the ship so deftly, to Claudette Morris for making the book real and Caitriona Horne and Louise Swannell for shouting about it.

Thank you to designer Nathan Burton and photographer Jamie Orlando Smith for capturing the Bread Street vibe. Thanks also to Phil Mundy and Olivia Wardle for making the food look so great.

Thank you to the team at the Gordon Ramsay Group who have made BSK a success in London and around the world. To my assistants, Michelle Prosser and Justin Mandel, and a special thank you to our CEO, Stuart Gillies, and Managing Director, Andy Wenlock. Thanks to Royal Doulton for the amazing Bread Street Kitchen line.

And lastly, thank you to my amazing family, my wife Tana, Megan, Jack, Holly and Matilda who inspire me every day.